Book 4

MAXIMIZE YOUR POTENTIAL

THROUGH THE POWER OF

YOUR SUBCONSCIOUS MIND

FOR

Health and Vitality

Other Hay House Classics Titles by Dr. Joseph Murphy

Believe in Yourself
Miracles of Your Mind
Techniques in Prayer Therapy

Other Books in the MAXIMIZE YOUR POTENTIAL Series:

❃ ❃ ❃

All of the above are available at your local bookstore,
or may be ordered by visiting:

Hay House USA: **www.hayhouse.com**®
Hay House Australia: **www.hayhouse.com.au**
Hay House UK: **www.hayhouse.co.uk**
Hay House South Africa: **www.hayhouse.co.za**
Hay House India: **www.hayhouse.co.in**

Book 4

MAXIMIZE YOUR POTENTIAL
THROUGH THE POWER OF
YOUR SUBCONSCIOUS MIND

FOR

Health and Vitality

One of a Series of Six Books
by
Dr. Joseph Murphy

Edited and Updated for the 21st Century
by Arthur R. Pell, Ph.D.

HAY HOUSE, INC.
Carlsbad, California • New York City
London • Sydney • Johannesburg
Vancouver • Hong Kong • New Delhi

DR. JOSEPH MURPHY

Maximize Your Potential Through the Power of Your Subconscious Mind for Health and Vitality is one of a series of six books by Joseph Murphy, D.D., Ph.D., edited and updated for the 21st century by Arthur R. Pell, Ph.D. Copyright © 2005 The James A. Boyer Revocable Trust. Exclusive worldwide rights in all languages available only through JMW Group Inc.

Published and distributed in the United States by: Hay House, Inc.: www.hay house.com • ***Published and distributed in Australia by:*** Hay House Australia Pty. Ltd.: www.hayhouse.com.au • ***Published and distributed in the United Kingdom by:*** Hay House UK, Ltd.: www.hayhouse.co.uk • ***Published and distributed in the Republic of South Africa by:*** Hay House SA (Pty), Ltd.: www.hayhouse.co.za • ***Distributed in Canada by:*** Raincoast: www.raincoast.com • ***Published in India by:*** Hay House Publishers India: www.hayhouse.co.in

Library of Congress Cataloging-in-Publication Data

Murphy, Joseph, 1898-1981
  Maximize your potential through the power of your subconscious mind for health and vitality / Joseph Murphy ; edited and updated for the 21st Century by Arthur R. Pell.
    p. cm.
  ISBN-13: 978-1-4019-1217-8 (tradepaper) 1. New Thought. I. Title.
  BF639.M8314 2005
  154.2--dc22
                                          2006035941

ISBN: 978-1-4019-1217-8

11 10 09 08 4 3 2 1
1st Hay House edition, May 2008

Printed in the United States of America

CONTENTS

———•—•———

Introduction to the Series

$\mathcal{W}$ake up and live! No one is destined to be unhappy or consumed with fear and worry, live in poverty, suffer ill health, and feel rejected and inferior. God created all humans in His image and has given us the power to overcome adversity and attain happiness, harmony, health, and prosperity.

You have within you the power to enrich your life! How to do this is no secret. It has been preached, written about, and practiced for millennia. You will find it in the works of the ancient philosophers, and all of the great religions have preached it. It is in the Hebrew scriptures, the Christian Gospels, Greek philosophy, the Muslim Koran, the Buddhist sutras, the Hindu Bhagavad Gita, and the writings of Confucius and Lao Tse. You will find it in the works of modern psychologists and theologians.

This is the basis of the philosophy of Dr. Joseph Murphy, one of the great inspirational writers and lecturers of the 20th century. He was not just a clergyman, but also a major figure in the modern interpretation of scriptures and other religious writings. As minister-director of the Church of Divine Science in Los Angeles, his lectures and sermons were attended by 1,300 to 1,500 people every Sunday, and millions tuned in to his daily radio program. He wrote more than 30 books, and his most well-known one, *The Power of the Unconscious Mind,* was first published in 1963 and became an immediate bestseller. It was acclaimed as one of the greatest self-help guides ever written. Millions of copies have, and continue to be, sold all over the world.

Following the success of this book, Dr. Murphy lectured to audiences of thousands in several countries. In his lectures he pointed out how real people have radically improved their lives by applying specific aspects of his concepts, and he provided practical guidelines on how all people can enrich themselves.

Dr. Murphy was a proponent of the New Thought movement, which was developed in the late 19th and early 20th century by many philosophers and deep thinkers who studied it and preached, wrote, and practiced a new way of looking at life. By combining metaphysical, spiritual, and pragmatic approaches to the way we think and live, they uncovered the secret for attaining what we truly desire.

This philosophy wasn't a religion in the traditional sense, but it was based on an unconditional belief in a higher being, an eternal presence: God. It was called by various names, such as "New Thought" and "New Civilization."

The proponents of New Thought or New Civilization preached a fresh idea of life that makes use of methods that lead to perfected results. They based their thinking on the concept that the human soul is connected with the atomic mind of universal substance, which links our lives with the universal law of supply, and we have the power to use it to enrich our lives. To achieve our goals, we must work, and through this working, we may suffer the thorns and heartaches of humankind. We can do all these things only as we have found the law and worked out an understanding of the principles that God seemed to have written in riddles in the past.

The New Thought concept can be summed up in these words:

You can become what you want to be.

All that we achieve and all that we fail to achieve is the direct result of our own thoughts. In a just and ordered universe, where loss of balance would mean total destruction, individual responsibility must be absolute. Our weaknesses, strengths, purity, and impurity are ours alone. They are brought about by ourselves and not by another. They can only be altered by ourselves, and never by anyone else. All of our happiness and suffering evolve from within. As we think, so we are; as we continue to think, so we remain. The only way we can rise, conquer, and achieve is by lifting up our thoughts. The only reason we may remain weak, abject, and miserable is to *refuse* to elevate our minds.

All achievements—whether in the business, intellectual, or spiritual world—are the result of definitely directed thought; and are governed by the same law and are reached by the same method. The only difference lies in the object of attainment. Those who would accomplish little must sacrifice little; those who would achieve much must sacrifice much; those who would attain a great deal must sacrifice a great deal.

New Thought means a new life: a way of living that is healthier, happier, and more fulfilling in every possible manner and expression.

Actually, there is nothing new in this, for it is as old and time-honored as humankind. It is novel to us when we discover the truths of life that set us free from lack, limitation, and unhappiness. At that moment, New Thought becomes a recurring, expanding awareness of the creative power within; of mind-principle; and of our Divine potential to be, to do, and to express more of our individual and natural abilities, aptitudes, and talents. The central mind-principle is that new thoughts, ideas, attitudes, and beliefs create new conditions. According to our beliefs, is it done unto us—good, bad, or indifferent. The essence of New Thought consists of the continual renewing of our mind, that we may manifest what is good, acceptable, and the perfect will of God.

To prove is to know surely, and to have trustworthy knowledge and experience. The truths of New Thought are practical, easy to demonstrate, and within the realm of accomplishment of everyone—if and when he or she chooses. All that is required is an open mind and a willing heart: open to hearing old truths presented in a different way; willing to change and to relinquish outmoded beliefs and to accept unfamiliar ideas and concepts—to have a higher vision of life, or a healing presence within.

The rebirth of our mind constitutes the entire purpose and practice of New Thought. Without this ongoing daily renewal, there can be no change. New Thought establishes and realizes an entirely new attitude and consciousness that inspires and enables us to enter into "life more abundant."

We have within us limitless powers to choose and to decide, and complete freedom to be conformed or to be transformed. To be conformed is to live according to that which already has taken or been given form—that which is visible and apparent to our own senses, including the ideas, opinions, beliefs, and edicts of others. It is to live and to be governed "by the fleeting and unstable fashions and conditions of the moment." The very word *conformed* suggests that our present environment has shape, and that we do not and should not deny its existence. All around us there are injustices, improprieties, and inequalities. We may and do find ourselves involved in them at times, and we should face them with courage and honesty and do our best to resolve them with the integrity and intelligence that we now possess.

Generally, the world accepts and believes that our environment is the cause of our present condition and circumstance—and the usual reaction and tendency is to drift into a state of acquiescence and quiet acceptance of the present. This is conformity of the worst kind: the consciousness of defeatism. It's worse because it is self-imposed. It is giving all power and attention to the outer, manifested state. New Thought insists on the renewal of the mind, and the recognition and acknowledgment of our responsibility in life—our ability to respond to the truths we now know.

One of the most active and effective of New Thought teachers, Charles Fillmore, co-founder of the Unity School of

Christianity, was a firm believer in personal responsibility. In his book *The Revealing Word,* he wrote (simply, and without equivocation): "Our consciousness is our real environment. The outer environment is always in correspondence to our consciousness."

Anyone who is open and willing to accept the responsibility has begun the transformation—the renewal of the mind that enables us to participate in our transformed life. "To transform" is "to change from one condition or state to another" (which is qualitatively better and more fulfilling) "from lack to abundance; loneliness to companionship; limitation to fullness; illness to vibrant health"—through this indwelling wisdom and power, the healing presence will remain within.

True and granted, there are some things we cannot change: the movement of the planets, the turn of the seasons, the pull of the oceans and tides, and the apparent rising and setting of the sun. Neither can we alter the minds and thoughts of another person—but we can change ourselves.

Who can prevent or inhibit the movement of your imagination and will? Only you can give that power to another. You can be transformed by the renewing of your mind. This is the key to a new life. You're a recording machine; and all the beliefs, impressions, opinions, and ideas accepted by you are impressed in your deeper subconscious. But you can change. You can begin now to fill your mind with noble and Godlike patterns of thoughts, and align yourself with the infinite spirit within. Claim beauty, love, peace, wisdom, creative ideas . . . and the infinite will respond accordingly, transforming your mind, body, and circumstances. Your thought is the medium between your spirit, your body, and the material world.

The transformation begins as we meditate, think upon, and absorb into our mentality those qualities that we desire to experience and express. Theoretical knowledge is good and necessary. We should understand what we're doing and why. However, actual change depends entirely on stirring up the gifts within—the invisible and intangible spiritual power given fully to every one of us.

This, and only this, ultimately breaks up and dissolves the very real claims and bondage of past unhappiness and distress. In addition, it heals the wounds of heartbreak and emotional pain. We all desire and require peace of mind—the greatest gift—in order to bring it into our environment. Mentally and emotionally, contemplate Divine peace, filling our mind and heart, our entire being. First say, "Peace be unto this house."

To contemplate lack of peace, disharmony, unhappiness, and discord, and expect peace to manifest is to expect the apple seed to grow into a pear. It makes little or no sense, and it violates all sense of reason, but it is the way of the world. We must seek ways to change our minds—to repent where necessary. As a result, renewal will occur, following naturally. It is desirable and necessary to transform our lives by ceasing to conform to the world's way of choosing or deciding, according to the events already formed and manifested.

The word *metaphysical* has become a synonym for the modern, organized movement. It was first used by Aristotle. Considered by some to have been his greatest writing, his 13th volume was simply entitled *Metaphysics.* The dictionary definition is: "Beyond natural science; the science of pure being." *Meta-* means "above, or beyond." *Metaphysics,* then, means "above or beyond physics"— "above or beyond the physical," the world of form. "Meta" is above that; it is the spirit of the mind, which is behind all things.

Biblically, the spirit of God is good. "They that worship God worship the spirit, or truth." When we have the spirit of goodness, truth, beauty, love, and goodwill, it is actually the Divine in us, moving through us. God, truth, life, energy, spirit—can it not be defined? How can it be? "To define it is to limit it."

This is expressed in a beautiful old meditation:

Ever the same in my innermost being: eternal, absolutely one, whole, complete, perfect; I AM indivisible, timeless, shapeless, ageless—without face, form, or figure. I AM the silent brooding presence, fixed in the hearts of all men (and women).

We must believe and accept that whatever we imagine and feel to be true will come to pass; whatever we desire for another, we are wishing for ourselves.

Emerson wrote: "We become what we think about all day long." In other words and most simply stated: Spirit, thought, mind, and meta is the expression of creative presence and power—and as in nature (physical laws), any force can be used two ways. For example, water can clean us or drown us; electricity can make life easier or more deadly. The Bible says: "I form the light, and create darkness; I make peace, and evil; I, the Lord, do all these things—I wound, I heal; I bless, I curse."

No angry deity is punishing us; we punish ourselves by misuse of the mind. We also are blessed (benefited) when we comprehend this fundamental principle and presence, and learn and accept a new thought or an entire concept.

Metaphysics, then, is the study of causation—concerned not with the effect that is now manifest, but rather with that which is causing the result. This discipline approaches spiritual ideas as scientists approach the world of form, just as they investigate the mind or causation from which the visible is formed, or derived. If a mind is changed, or a cause is changed, the effect is changed.

The strength and beauty of metaphysics, in my opinion, is that it is not confined to any one particular creed, but is universal. One can be a Jew, Christian, Muslim, or Buddhist and yet still be a metaphysician.

There are poets, scientists, and philosophers who claim no creed; their belief is metaphysical.

Jesus was a master metaphysician—he understood the mind and employed it to lift up, inspire, and heal others.

When Mahatma Gandhi (the "great-souled" one) was asked what his religion was, he replied, "I am a Christian . . . a Jew . . . a Buddhist . . . a Hindu . . . I AM all these things."

The term *New Thought* has become a popular, generalized term. Composed of a very large number of churches, centers, prayer groups, and institutions, this has become a metaphysical movement that reveals the oneness or unity of humankind with infinite life . . . with the innate dignity, worth, or value of every individual. In fact, and in truth, the emphasis is on the individual rather than on an organizational body or function. But as mentioned, there is nothing new in New Thought. Metaphysics is actually the oldest of all religious approaches. It reveals our purpose to express God, and the greater measures of the Good: "I AM come to bring you life and that more abundantly." It reveals our identity: "children of the infinite" who are loved and have spiritual value as necessary parts of the Creative Holy (whole) One.

Metaphysics enables and assists us to return to our Divine Source, and ends the sense of separation and feeling of alienation; of wandering in a barren, unfriendly desert wasteland. This approach has always been, is now, and ever will be available to all—patiently waiting our discovery and revelation.

Many thousands have been introduced to New Thought through one or another of its advocates. Its formation was gradual, and usually considered to have begun with Phineas P. Quimby. In a fascinating article in *New Thought* magazine, Quimby wrote about his work in 1837. After experimenting with mesmerism for a period of years, he concluded that it was not the hypnotism itself, but the conditioning of the subconscious, which led to the resulting changes. Although Quimby had very little formal education, he had a brilliant, investigative mind and was an original thinker. In addition, he was a prolific writer and diarist. Records have been published detailing the development of his findings. He eventually became a wonderful student of the Bible and duplicated two-thirds of the Old and New Testament healings. He found that there was much confusion about the true meaning of many biblical passages, which caused misunderstanding and misinterpretation of Jesus Christ.

All through the 20th century, so many inspired teachers, authors, ministers, and lecturers contributed to the New Thought movement. Dr. Charles E. Braden, of the University of Chicago, called these people "spirits in rebellion" because these men and women were truly breaking free from existing dogmatism, rituals, and creeds. (Rebelling at inconsistencies in the old traditions led some individuals to fear religion.) Dr. Braden became discontent with the status quo and refused to conform any longer.

New Thought is an individual practice of the truths of life—a gradual, continuing process. We can learn a bit today, and even more tomorrow. Never will we experience a point where there is nothing more to be discovered. It is infinite, boundless, and eternal. We have all the time we need—eternity. Many of us are impatient with ourselves, and with what we consider our failures. Looking back, though, we discover that these have been periods of learning, and we needn't make these mistakes again. Progress may seem ever so slow: "In patience, possess ye your soul."

In Dr. Murphy's book *Pray Your Way Through It: The Revelation,* he commented that heaven was noted as being "awareness," and Earth, "manifestation." Your new heaven is your revised point of view—your new dimension of consciousness. When we see—that is, see spiritually, we then realize that in the absolute, all is blessed, harmony, boundless love, wisdom, complete peace, and perfection. Identify with these truths, calm the sea of fear; have confidence and faith, and become stronger and surer.

In the books in this series, Dr. Murphy has synthesized the profundities of this power and has put them into an easily understood and pragmatic form so that you can apply them immediately to your life. As Dr. Murphy was a Protestant minister, many of his examples and citations come from the Bible. The concepts these passages illustrate should not be viewed as sectarian. Indeed, their messages are universal and are preached in most religions and philosophies. He often reiterated that the essence of knowledge is in the law of life and belief. It is not Catholic, Protestant, Muslim, or Hindu; it is pure and simple faith: "Do unto others accordingly."

Dr. Murphy's wife, Dr. Jean Murphy, continued his ministry after his death in 1981. In a lecture she gave in 1986, quoting her late husband, she reiterated his philosophy:

> I want to teach men and women of their Divine Origin, and the powers regnant within them. I want to inform them that this power is within and that they are their own saviors and capable of achieving their own salvation. This is the message of the Bible, and nine-tenths of our confusion today is due to wrongful, literal interpretation of the life-transforming truths offered in it.
>
> I want to reach the majority, the man on the street, the woman overburdened with duty and suppression of her talents and abilities. I want to help others at every stage or level of consciousness to learn of the wonders within.

She said of her husband: "He was a practical mystic, possessed by the intellect of a scholar, the mind of a successful executive, the heart of the poet." His message summed up was: "You are the king, the ruler of your world, for you are one with God."

Joseph Murphy was a firm believer that it was God's plan for people to be healthy, prosperous, and happy. He countered those theologians and others who claimed that desire is evil and urged people to crush it. He said that extinction of our longings means apathy—no feeling, no action. He preached that desire is a gift of God. It is healthy and wholesome to want to become more and better than we were yesterday . . . in the areas of health, abundance, companionship, security, and more. How could these be wrong?

Desire is behind all progress. Without it, nothing would be accomplished. It is the creative power and must be channeled constructively. For example, if one is poor, yearning for wealth wells up from within; if one is ill, there is a wish for health; if lonely, there is a desire for companionship and love.

We must believe that we can improve our lives. A belief—whether it is true, false, or merely indifferent—sustained over a period of time becomes assimilated and is incorporated into our mentality. Unless countermanded by faith of an opposite nature, sooner or later it takes form and is expressed or experienced as fact, form, condition, circumstance, and the events of life. We have the power within us to change negative beliefs to positive ones, and thereby change ourselves for the better.

You give the command and your subconscious mind will faithfully obey it. You will get a reaction or response according to the nature of the thought you hold in your conscious mind. Psychologists and psychiatrists point out that when thoughts are conveyed to your subconscious mind, impressions are made in your brain cells. As soon as this part of you accepts any idea, it proceeds to put it into effect immediately. It works by association of ideas and uses every bit of knowledge that you have gathered in your lifetime to bring about its purpose. It draws on the infinite power, energy, and wisdom within you, lining up all the laws of nature to get its way. Sometimes it seems to bring about an immediate solution to your difficulties, but at other times it may take days, weeks, or longer.

The habitual thinking of your conscious mind establishes deep grooves in your subconscious mind. This is very favorable for you if your recurring thoughts are harmonious, peaceful, and constructive. On the other hand, if you have indulged in fear, worry, and other destructive concepts, the remedy is to recognize the omnipotence of your subconscious and decree freedom, happiness, perfect health, and prosperity. Your subconscious mind, being creative and one with your Divine source, will proceed to create the freedom and happiness that you have earnestly declared.

Now for the first time, Dr. Murphy's lectures have been combined, edited, and updated in six new books that bring his teachings into the 21st century. To enhance and augment this original text, we have incorporated material from some of Jean Murphy's lectures and have added examples of people whose success reflects Dr. Murphy's philosophy.

The other works in this series are listed on the second page of this book, but just reading them will not improve your state of being. To truly maximize your potential, you must study these principles, take them to heart, integrate them into your mentality, and apply them as an integral part of your approach to every aspect of your life.

— **Arthur R. Pell, Ph.D.**, editor

☧ ☧

Editor's Note: While updating these works, at times I have added current examples (that is, events and situations that may have occurred after Joseph Murphy's death) showing how basic principles presented by the author are still valid.

Preface

Since ancient times, people have strived to attain the ideal: a sound body and mind. This is because good health is a prerequisite for a good life. You should lay a foundation for your health just as you establish anything of importance—by studying and adopting the sanest and the most scientific methods. You should think, read, and talk about health just as a law student should think, read, and talk about law.

You must firmly hold to the conviction that it's natural and right to remain young. Constantly repeat to yourself that it's wrong and wicked for you to grow old in appearance. Weakness and decrepitude couldn't have been in the Creator's plan for humankind, for we're made in His image of perfection. Clearly, becoming ill or incapacitated must be the result of wrong training and thinking.

It's your responsibility to take care of your body. You must make it a high priority to eat nourishing foods, maintain an exercise program that will keep your muscles toned and your body strong, and eliminate smoking and other health-draining habits from your life.

You aren't old until you lose your curiosity and your heart becomes weary and unresponsive. As long as you're involved in life in many ways, you can't grow old in spirit. You only become feeble (no matter how many birthdays you've had), when you've lost touch with the youth, ideals, and spirit of your times . . . when you've ceased to grow and learn.

The idea that our energy must begin to decline and that the fires of ambition will die out after we reach a certain age has a most pernicious influence upon the mind, for it's impossible for us to go beyond our self-imposed limits and do what we really believe we can't. Therefore, constantly affirm: "I am always well and always young. I cannot grow old except by producing the condition of old age through my thoughts."

Keep in mind Dr. Murphy's prescription for keeping young, realizing that living should be a perpetual joy. Youth and happiness are synonymous. If you don't enjoy life, feel that it's a delight to be alive, and look upon your work as a grand privilege, you'll age prematurely.

Always maintain a happy mental attitude. If you live this ideal, the aging processes can't get ahold of you. Every time you think of yourself, create a vivid mental picture of your ideal self as vibrant, healthy, and vigorous. Feel the spirit of youth and hope surging through your body.

We can find the elixir of youth, which chemists have long sought, in *ourselves*. The secret is in our own mentality. Perpetual rejuvenation is possible only through right thinking. We look as old as we think and feel because it's our thoughts and feelings that change our appearance.

In this book, Dr. Murphy stresses the importance of having faith that God wants you to be healthy and vital. He demonstrates over and over again how positive belief leads to healing and the maintenance of an energetic and happy life.

As Dr. Murphy points out, the power to heal yourself lies within you. As in all of his books, he reiterates that your subconscious governs your actions and reactions. If you feed it with negative thoughts of ill health, deterioration, and senility, your body will experience these things. However, if you use prayer and meditation to program your deeper mind with thoughts of good health, vitality, and youthfulness, your body will manifest these qualities.

This doesn't mean that prayer alone will keep you well or cure your ailments. The body God has given you must also be properly cared for. You have an obligation to keep your body in tip-top shape by developing good habits. Faith and prayer can't overcome your neglect of good hygiene, nutrition, or exercise; but they can enable you to gain the strength of mind to take the necessary steps to correct and overcome the bad habits that debilitate your body.

As Dr. Murphy was a minister of a Christian denomination, he drew many of his examples from the Bible. In the following chapters, he cites several passages from the New Testament that describe healings performed by Jesus. Dr. Murphy's interpretations of these wonderful events can provide meaning and inspiration to all readers. Adherents to other religions or philosophical creeds can appreciate and learn from these parables. Similar examples of great healings are found in the writings of most religions, as well as in nonsectarian sources.

As you read this book, resolve to make changes in your lifestyle to maximize your potential to create a sound body and mind.

— **Arthur R. Pell, Ph.D.**, editor

Chapter One

Good Health—It's Up to You

*I*t's pitiable to see young people who start out in life with the ambition to make a name for themselves ruin the possibility of doing anything great by sacrificing their health—the very thing upon which they're most dependent for the attainment of their goals.

Do you realize what splendid capital for success there is in good health and a strong, vigorous constitution that's able to withstand any amount of grueling work and hard knocks? Have you ever considered that having the physical reserves to keep going in the face of a long, persistent strain has carried many people through difficult times and trying conditions, while weaker individuals would have completely succumbed?

We can succeed without financial capital, but not without physical and mental vitality. After all, no defective machine can turn out good work. To accomplish great things in the world, we must possess a healthy body; otherwise, everything we do will bear the stamp of weakness.

Robust health quadruples the efficiency and power of every human faculty and function. It clears the cobwebs from the brain, improves judgment, increases energy, and refreshes the cells in every tissue of the body. In contrast, a muddled, exhausted brain is incapable of doing good work, thinking clearly, or planning effectively. Bodies that are worn out by bad habits—including a lack of sleep and recreation—can't do good work.

When you find yourself becoming morose and despondent and lose your former zest for living, you can be pretty sure that you need more sleep, a trip to the country, or at least some outdoor exercise. If you get these, you'll find that all your old enthusiasm will return. A few days rambling in the hills and meadows will erase the dark pictures that haunt you and will restore buoyancy to your animal spirits.

With good health and strong determination, you can accomplish wonderful things. However, no matter how much ambition you may have, if you ruin your health by having bad habits, you destroy your hopes of achieving anything important. It's true that there are examples of people in poor health—even invalids—who've done quite remarkable things . . . but think what these people might have accomplished if they'd had strong, vigorous constitutions! Ill health is a perpetual handicap, and the greater your ambition, the greater the disappointment the inability to reach your goals will cause. On the other hand, excellent health increases the efficiency and power of every faculty and multiplies your brainpower many times over, giving you a keener edge. People with only one talent but superb health often accomplish a great deal more than those with dozens of abilities but poor health.

There are young people of unusual ability, fine education, and good training who can't make much headway in their careers because they aren't able to work more than two or three hours a day. They don't have the vitality or the strength for sustained effort. Their physical reservoirs become exhausted so quickly that they can't successfully enter the strenuous competitions of the day. They're constantly mortified and chagrined because those who don't have half their mental ability, but possess twice their physical stamina, outstrip them.

Many people greatly reduce their chances for success by developing bad habits that waste most of their energy. Perhaps 10 percent disappears in drink, and another 10 percent goes up in smoke. They may squander another 25 percent of their energy reserves trying to have a good time, and an additional 10 percent in idleness and shiftless behavior. Many lose quite a large percentage of their stamina fretting and worrying. As a result, they come to their tasks with jaded power and exhausted faculties. In fact, some individuals bring hardly 5 percent of their potential energy and ability to their great life tasks and work.

In order to do big things, you must keep your mind fresh and responsive. When your faculties are sharp and energized, you can do more effective work in a few hours than workaholics will accomplish in 12 or 14. Many have lost their power to produce by forcing their brain to work too many hours each day.

Thousands of people would achieve vastly more if they'd get out of their offices, factories, or other places of business earlier; work fewer hours; and make more time for exercise and recreation. In short, keeping oneself in great health is the best possible investment.

Make it a rule to go to your job every morning feeling fresh and vigorous. You want to be strong, vibrant, and filled with creative energy.

⛬

Most people seem to think that health is determined by fate or that it's largely a question of heredity. This is illogical, for everyone has the power of choice and can take actions to improve their stamina and health. Nonetheless, few make the effort to do so. The same individuals who spend years educating themselves and preparing for a career barely give a thought to what they can do to better care for their bodies.

When we realize that robust health multiplies our power of initiative, increases our creative ability, generates enthusiasm and spontaneity, and strengthens the quality of our judgment and decisions, we'll be more diligent in our care of our physical bodies.

⛬

Health can be established only by focusing on wellness instead of disease, strength instead of weakness, harmony instead of discord, truth instead of error, and love instead of hatred. We need to fill our minds with thoughts that build us up rather than those that tear us down. We rejuvenate our bodies by renewing our thoughts.

Confidence is a powerful factor in health, and we should thoroughly believe in our ability to keep ourselves well through harmonious, positive thinking. As long as we dwell on disease, physical weakness, and genetic tendencies, it will be impossible to develop a strong, healthy body.

⛬

A well-balanced, disciplined intellect acts powerfully upon the physical self and tends to bring it into harmony. On the other hand, a weak, vacillating, and ignorant mind will ultimately lead the body into chaos. Every thought tends to reproduce itself, and ghastly mental pictures of illness and vice of all sorts produce leprosy in the soul, which then reproduces them in the body. The mind devours everything that's brought to it—the good *and* the bad—and it will produce soundness or rottenness, beauty or deformity, harmony or discord, and truth or error according to the quality of the thoughts we feed it.

Virtue, holiness, pure thoughts, high ideals, noble living, generosity, charity, and an unselfish love for humanity all tend to lengthen life, while their opposites tend to shorten it.

A happy person is likely to be healthy. When you find your place in life and are doing work that you love, you're both healthier and happier. Who hasn't seen people of indifferent health—perhaps even invalids—suddenly develop a sound body when they're doing something they love and achieve some success in that area?

Few people realize that their ailments are largely self-induced. They get into a habit of not feeling well. If they wake up in the morning with a slight headache or some other trifling indisposition, instead of trying to rise above this condition, they take positive pleasure in discussing their pain with anyone who will listen. Instead of combating the tendency to illness by filling their lungs with pure, fresh air, they dose themselves with headache tablets or some other patent medicine advertised to cure whatever malady they think they have. They begin to pity themselves and try to attract sympathy from others. Unconsciously, by detailing and dwelling upon their symptoms, they reinforce the first simple suggestions of illness with an entire army of thoughts, fears, and images of disease until they're ultimately unable to do a day's work.

Some people become overly concerned when faced with minor illnesses or aches and pains and fall back into bed to pamper themselves. They moan, "I don't feel up to going to work." However, it's necessary to train yourself to follow through on your tasks whether you like them or not.

What if business executives, who are compelled to work all day and have neither the time nor the opportunity to coddle themselves when they feel low, were to become slaves to their whims and fancies? Suppose they said to themselves, "I'm likely to be ill this summer and am going to prepare for the worst. I shall have a couch put into my office so that I can lie down when I feel bad, and I'll buy a stock of medicine in order to be ready for any emergency."

People with common sense would consider it a disgrace even to entertain such thoughts. They know that if they were to act in this way, their business would soon collapse. They also know from experience that it's not wise to give up every time they don't feel like doing something.

Suppose that a general found his soldiers lounging about the camp, lying under trees, and taking it easy because they didn't feel like doing drills and had decided to wait until they felt inspired. What kind of an army would he have? What kind of discipline? The soldiers must fall into line and commence the drills at the appointed minute whether they feel like it or not. If they're really sick, they must go to the doctor, but if they're not ill enough to be in the hospital or under a physician's care, they must do their drills.

❧✠❧

The moment you allow yourself to be governed by your moods, you open the door to a host of enemies of your health, success, and happiness. Therefore, don't sympathize with sick, diseased, or lazy thoughts under any circumstance. If you yield once to such thoughts, before you know it, you may become their slave.

Some people actually attract illness to themselves by constantly thinking about it. They feel sure that if they get their feet wet, they'll soon be sick with pneumonia or influenza. If they happen to sit in a draft for a few minutes, they're confident that dire results will follow and that they'll get a cold or sore throat. If they cough a little, they have dreadful visions of developing some lung disease. *Doesn't that run in the family?* they think to themselves. They fix images of sickness in the mind and thereby lessen its power to resist disease, making the body more susceptible to the very things they fear.

The best safeguard you can give yourself is a determination that you'll be the master of yourself and that you won't be dictated to by your moods or whims of any kind. You'll find that if you expect great things of yourself, always exact a high standard, and accept no apologies or excuses from Mr. Liver or Mrs. Stomach, your health will be better and you'll accomplish infinitely more than if you allow your feelings to hold you in subjugation.

It doesn't take a great deal of practice to be able to throw off any ordinary symptoms of indisposition by focusing firmly on opposing thoughts of health and cheerfulness. Insist that you won't give up and that you'll do your day's work to the best of your ability, and it's probable that before the morning is half over, you'll feel better. Every thought that you have is inscribed in your brain, where it filters down into your subconscious and determines how your body responds. This isn't a theory—it's a fact.

People have died because they thought they were terribly hurt when, in fact, no wound existed. For example, a man who thought he'd swallowed a tack had horrible symptoms, including a painful swelling in his throat, until he discovered that he hadn't actually ingested an object.

There are hundreds of other cases in which belief alone produced great suffering and even death. On the other hand, sickness and disease can evaporate in the face of excitement, great joy, or even alarm. For example, when Benvenuto Cellini was about to cast his famous statue of Perseus, he suddenly developed a fever and was forced to go home to bed. In the midst of Cellini's suffering, one of his workmen rushed in and exclaimed, "Oh, Benvenuto, your statue is spoiled, and there's no hope whatsoever of saving it!"

Cellini got dressed hastily and rushed to his furnace, where he found that his metal cast had "caked." Ordering more dry oak, he fired the furnace, worked fiercely in the falling rain, and saved his cast.

Cellini said, "After all was over, I turned to a plate of salad on a bench there and ate with a hearty appetite and drank, together with the whole crew. Afterward I retired to my bed—healthy and happy—and slept as sweetly as though I'd never felt a touch of illness." His overpowering hope of saving his statue drove away his illness, leaving him in perfect health.

The wonder is that humanity has taken so long to understand this power of the mind over the body and apply it. Like electricity, the power of the mind has always existed, but is only just now beginning to be recognized and used.

⸺✤⸺

Physicians recognize the role the mind plays in curing disease, and entire books have been written documenting cases in which mental power has been more effective than medicine or surgery. As one of the fathers of modern medicine, Sir William Osler, wrote:

> The physical method has always played an important, though largely unrecognized, part in therapeutics. It is from faith, which buoys up the spirits, sets the blood flowing more freely and the nerves playing their part without disturbance, that a large part of all cure arises. Despondency, or lack of faith, will often sink the stoutest constitution almost to death's door; faith will enable a

spoonful of water or a bread pill to do almost miracles of healing when the best medicines have been given over in despair. The basis of the entire profession of medicine is faith in the doctor, his drugs, and his methods.

Similarly, psychiatrist and neurologist Smith Ely Jelliffe noted:

The power to heal by faith is not the special property of any sect or class, nor the exclusive right of any system. Belief in gods and goddesses, prayer to idols of wood and stone, faith in the doctor, and belief in ourselves engendered from within or without—these are all expressions of the great therapeutic value for healing that resides in the influence of mental states on bodily functions. These will not move mountains or cure consumption; they will not influence a broken leg nor an organic paralysis; but suggestion, in its various forms, may be and is, one of the strongest aids to all therapeutic measures. Of its abuse by designing hypnotists, blackmailers, clairvoyants, and a motley crew of parasites, space does not permit particularization. The human mind is credulous—it believes what it wants or wills to believe—and the use of suggestion in therapeutics is one of great power for good and for evil.

⊰✦⊱

Few people realize how much their health depends upon the saneness of their thinking. Indeed, you can't hold thoughts about disease in your mind without having them manifest in the body. Harmony can't exist in the body if there's disease in the mind.

As an experiment, try thinking of yourself as an absolutely perfect being, possessing superb health, a magnificent body, a vigorous constitution, a sublime mind, and the capacity to withstand any amount of strain. Never allow yourself to have a defective, crippled ideal of yourself—don't entertain such an imperfect health model for an instant—for these mental patterns will gradually be reproduced in your physical condition.

Librarians report that there's an astonishing demand among readers for medical books. Many people who imagine that they have a particular disease often develop a morbid curiosity or desire to read everything they can find about the subject. When they discover—as they frequently do—that they have some of the symptoms of the disease they're reading about, the conviction that they're ill is fastened still more deeply in their minds. The strength of this belief is often their greatest hindrance to a cure.

We should avoid dwelling upon our ailments or studying our symptoms. Physicians tell us that "self-diagnosers" who constantly analyze themselves and are forever on the alert for the least symptom of disease can never enjoy perfect health. We must instead keep a high ideal of health in our mind and fight every discordant thought and enemy of harmony as we would combat a temptation to commit a crime. We must never affirm or repeat something about our health that we don't wish to be true.

Nervous people with vivid imaginations rarely see life in a perfectly sane way. They're very apt to become morbid and make mountains out of molehills. They exaggerate every little ache or pain and interpret them as a symptom of something worse to come. If their relatives died of arteriosclerosis, cancer, or any other of the dread diseases, the conviction that they're likely to develop one or the other of these maladies hangs like a pall over their lives, seriously impairs their health, and paralyzes their efficiency.

What a terrible thing to go through life with such a nightmare staring you in the face! How foolish to live with the specter of death constantly by your side . . . to drag through the years with the belief that you're not going to live long and that you carry the seeds of a terrible disease that's likely to develop at any moment.

Think of a person spending years getting a college education and training for a career, all the time haunted by the possibility that he or she may be thwarted by the development of some ghastly hereditary disease that could result in a premature death. It would be enough to kill the ambition of a Napoléon.

There are people in delicate health who habitually hold sick and discordant thoughts in their minds. They're always thinking and talking about their ailments. They gloat over their symptoms, watch them, and study them until they develop the problems they expect. According to the law of mind, like produces like; it can't produce anything else.

Many individuals not only cripple their efficiency but keep themselves sick by constantly feeding their minds negative suggestions such as, "I don't feel well today," "I feel miserable," "I'm weak," "I'm sick," or "It's flu season."

If you keep saying to yourself, "I'm wretched, weak, and sick" or "I always feel run down," how can you expect to become strong and well? Health and vigor will never come to you if you perpetually harp upon your weakness and pity yourself because of your poor health. Health is integrity, wholeness, and completeness. If you talk about anything else, you'll get that instead.

Imagine that you're an attorney pleading the cause of your health. Summon up every bit of evidence you can possibly find. Don't give your case away to your opponent. Instead, plead it vigorously with all the strength you can command. You'll be surprised to see how your body will respond to such energetic affirmations.

One time a physician passing through a ward thoughtlessly said to the nurse in a voice loud enough for the patient to overhear, "That man won't live." The patient happened to know about the power of the mind as a restorative, and said to the nurse with great emphasis, "I *will* live."And he did completely recover.

We don't realize how much we weaken ourselves and destroy our resistance to disease by focusing on ideas of physical debilitation. When we learn that the mind is its own tonic, we won't need narcotics or drugs of any kind. It's only a question of holding harmonious, loving thoughts; when these dominate the mind, enemy thoughts that tear down and destroy health can't enter.

At the end of the day, we should be able to turn off all the busy thought processes that exhaust the nerves and drain the brain of energy. Then we can begin to recuperate for the next day and regenerate our vital forces. If we could always keep in our minds the ideal of complete health, wholeness, and perfection, there would be no room to harbor sickly, weak thoughts.

In a Nutshell

With robust health and strong determination, you can accomplish wonderful things; however, no matter how much ambition you have, if you ruin your health through bad habits, you cut off your greatest chance for accomplishing anything important.

It's your responsibility to take care of your body. You must make it a high priority to eat the proper foods and maintain an exercise program that will keep your muscles toned and your body strong. You need to make it a point to only drink alcoholic beverages in moderation and eliminate smoking and other health-draining habits from your life.

Health can be established only by thinking about wellness instead of disease, strength instead of weakness, harmony instead of discord, truth instead of error, and love instead of hatred. A strong physical self is developed by focusing on constructive thoughts rather than those that tear us down.

A conviction that we should be master of ourselves under all conditions will protect us from many of the ills to which we fall victim. If we think diseased thoughts, we attract sickness. If we think healthy thoughts, we attract health.

Try to remember that truth, health, and harmony aren't far away from you but are always with you—*in* you. Realizing that they're always present will greatly help you.

There are people in delicate health who habitually hold in their minds sick and discordant thoughts. They're always thinking and talking about their ailments. They gloat over their symptoms, study them, and look for them until they have the problems they expect, for like produces like.

Thinking about health instead of disease could cure many invalids since positive thought is the greatest panacea in the world.

As long as you hold a youthful, vigorous, energetic, creative ideal in your mind, your body responds by creating excellent health.

Chapter Two

---·•·---

Developing Your Healing
Consciousness

*I*n the preceding chapter, you learned about the importance of developing good health habits and conditioning your mind to think positive, life-giving thoughts. If you truly believe that you're healthy, you will be. This isn't a new or modern concept: It was preached and demonstrated in ancient times and in many religions.

There's only One Healing Power, although it's called by many names, such as God, Infinite Healing Presence, Divine Love, Providence, Nature, and the Life Principle. In the Bible, this Power is called "Father." It's the healing agent for all diseases, whether they're mental, emotional, or physical. It directs your subconscious and can heal your mind and body and all illnesses and impediments. This Healing Power responds to you regardless of your race, creed, or color. It doesn't care whether you belong to a church or have any religious affiliations.

You've had hundreds of healings since you were a child. You can recall how the Presence mended your cuts, burns, bruises, contusions, sprains, and so on. In all probability, you didn't have to apply any external remedies—the innate Power within the body knew just what to do.

When Susan K. came to see me, she was extremely upset. Her daughter had been diagnosed with an unusual ailment and was running a high fever. The doctor had administered drugs and shots, but nothing seemed to help. Susan told me that she and her husband were in the process of getting divorced and that she felt terribly distraught. I explained to her that she was subconsciously communicating these feelings of distress to her child, who naturally became ill. Children are at the mercy of their parents and are highly influenced by the dominant mental and emotional atmosphere that surrounds them. They haven't yet reached the age of reason, when they can take control of their thoughts, emotions, and reactions to life.

I suggested that Susan relieve her tension by reading the 23rd Psalm and by praying for the peace and harmony of her husband. She poured out love and goodwill to him and overcame her anger. Having quieted her own mind, she began to pray for her child in this manner: "Spirit is the life of my daughter. Spirit has no temperature. It is never sick or feverish. The peace of God flows through my child's mind and body. The harmony, health, love, and perfection of God are made manifest in every atom of her body. She is relaxed and serene. I am now stirring up the gift of God within her, and all is well."

Susan repeated the above prayer every hour for several hours. Shortly thereafter, she noticed a remarkable change in her daughter, who awakened and asked for a doll and something to eat. Her temperature became normal. What had happened? The little girl became well because her mom was no longer feverish or agitated in her mind. The child instantly felt her mood of peace, harmony, and love, and a corresponding reaction was produced.

We're all natural healers for the simple reason that the Healing Presence of God is within everyone and responds to everyone. We can contact It with our thoughts, so don't let the word *incurable* frighten you. Realize that you're dealing with the Creative Intelligence that made your body. Although some people will say that healing is impossible, be assured that the Infinite Healing Presence is instantly available. You can always draw on Its power through the creative law of your own mind. Make use of the Divine Source now to perform miracles in your life. With God, all things are possible. *I will restore health unto thee, and I will heal thee of thy wounds, saith the Lord.*

Through the Infinite Healing Presence, you can bring into your life anything you wish.

Millions of people who profess to be religious often make statements such as "My child is incurable," "It's hopeless," or "I can't be healed." At the same time, they say that with God, all things are possible. They're contradicting themselves. In fact, when you deny the Infinite Healing Presence, you're thinking like an atheist. God created the body from a cell, knows all of its processes and functions, and certainly can heal it. *Surely, He that hath made the eye, can He not see? He that hath made the ear, can He not hear?*

You may use the Infinite Presence for any purpose, not just for healing the body or the mind. It's the same Power that attracts the ideal husband or wife into your life, prospers you in business, and reveals answers to your most difficult problems. Through the correct application of the law of mind, you can become a great salesperson, musician, artist, or surgeon. You can also use Infinite Intelligence to replace discord with harmony, pain with peace, sadness with joy, and poverty with abundance.

There are three steps in the healing process. The first is not to be afraid of the condition that ails you. The second is to realize that the condition is only the product of past thinking, which will have no more power as you continue to do spiritual affirmations. The third step is to mentally exalt the miraculous Healing Power of God within you.

Follow these three steps, and they'll instantly stop the production of all mental poisons in you or in the person for whom you're praying. Your thoughts and feelings will soon be made manifest. Don't allow yourself to be swayed by human opinion and worldly fears, but live in the belief that God is in action in your mind and body. As the Bible says: "The kingdom of heaven is at hand. Heal the sick, cleanse the lepers, raise the dead, cast out demons. Freely you have received, freely give."

Poor health is a lack of oneness with God. It indicates a separation from the Divine. However, you can restore your subconscious to wholeness, beauty, peace, and serenity by filling your conscious mind with life-giving patterns of harmony, health, and right action. Teach your mind to give up its illusions, resentment, and antagonism. You can't be healed when you're obsessed with resentment, hatred, and self-condemnation. It's impossible. You must give up all of these false ideas and accept that the kingdom of heaven is at hand and that you're an expression of God's intelligence, wisdom, power, and boundless love.

Wish for everyone what you desire for yourself: health, happiness, peace, and all the blessings of life. Forgive yourself for harboring negative thoughts and absolve everyone you think has hurt you. Then you create a vacuum, and the Holy Spirit of God will rush in and heal you. Accept the fact that the Spirit in you is God. It's the Only Cause, and you therefore shouldn't give power to external things—to the weather, politicians, your neighbors, germs, or anything else. Change your mind, and you'll transform your body.

Fill your mind with the truths of God, and you'll crowd out everything unlike Him. It's like putting drops of clean water into a pail of dirty water. If you have patience, you'll eventually have a bucket of clear water to drink. When you fill your mind with eternal verities—whatever is true, lovely, noble, and good—you'll obliterate from your subconscious everything unlike God, and healing will take place. Your positive thoughts are like spiritual penicillin that destroys the bacteria of fear, worry, and anxiety.

Persistence and repetition work miracles. Reiterate the great truths, such as:

The Healing Power of God is now flowing through me, healing me, and making me whole. The Infinite Presence made me and It knows how to heal. It understands all the processes and functions of my body. I claim that the Holy Spirit is flowing through me now, animating, sustaining, healing, and restoring my entire being to wholeness, beauty, and perfection.

The Healing Presence restores your soul, which is your subconscious. No matter what the problem is, it's just a negative pattern lodged in the recesses of your deeper mind. Since the lower is subject to the higher, as you "emotionalize" your thoughts and feed your subconscious with life-giving patterns of wholeness, beauty, and perfection, it has no alternative but to be cleansed. Then healing will follow.

It's useless to petition God and beg for healing. God doesn't respond to your beseeching or supplication but to your belief and conviction. *According to your belief, it is done unto you.*

Healing follows a real change of mind and heart. Announce the kingdom of heaven to your own mind. Teach your subconscious to give up fear, hate, resentment, and false beliefs and to not judge according to appearances. Don't give power to external conditions, but to the Divine Spirit within you, allowing It to flow through you.

If you have a poor view of yourself, you'll be sick, frustrated, and neurotic. On the other hand, if you envision yourself as successful and whole, seeing the doctor congratulating you on your perfect health, your vision will manifest. When you regularly, systematically, and vigorously reiterate to your mind that the kingdom of harmony, health, peace, wisdom, beauty, and boundless love are all within you, then your vision will soar, your faith will be kindled, and healings will unfold in your life. *All things be ready if the mind be so.*

Some people come to me complaining that they're haunted by voices that periodically make them do malicious acts. They say that these voices won't leave them alone and that they can't suppress them, even through prayer or reading the Bible. They're convinced that these messages come from supernatural beings or departed spirits who've taken possession of their minds. In fact, their subconscious minds have become dominated and controlled by an all-potent, negative thought. Although the subconscious possesses transcendent powers, it's amenable to both positive and harmful suggestions. To overcome this, they must reprogram their subconscious with constructive, harmonious thoughts.

I recommend to these individuals that they memorize the following meditation and repeat it several times a day:

God's love, peace, harmony, and wisdom flood my mind and heart. I love the truth, I hear the truth, and I know the truth. I know that God is love, and His compassion surrounds and enfolds me. God's river of peace floods my mind, and I give thanks for my freedom.

I suggest that they say this prayer slowly, reverently, and with deep feeling, particularly prior to going to sleep. By identifying themselves with harmony and peace, they change the thought patterns and imagery in their minds, and healing follows.

Phineas Parkhurst Quimby, one of the early proponents of mental healing, stated over a hundred years ago that the body acts as it's acted upon. It's composed of primordial substance and is molded by thought. It has no initiative or volition in and of itself, but instead manifests according to the thoughts that you feed it. For example, suppose that your thoughts are full of fear, anxiety, and worry. You may very well get gastritis, which is an inflammation of the stomach, or ulcers. Modern physicians today tell us that negative emotions can provoke all kinds of disease. If you have your ulcers excised by a surgeon but continue to fret, fume, and fulminate, even though you stick with a bland diet, you'll get ulcers again. Therefore, surgery isn't really the answer—a change of mind is. Thousands of people are being healed of various illnesses by filling their minds with the truth of God, focusing on peace and harmony, and thinking about whatever is just, lovely, pure, and good.

⊶✝⊷

There's no such thing as an incurable disease. There are only incurable people who believe that they can't be healed. Many people have been healed of malignancies, while others haven't because of the intensity of the fear buried in their subconscious mind.

⊶✝⊷

The consciousness of love is the greatest healing power in the world. There are many people who have little formal education and no knowledge of anatomy or physiology, but they have an immense consciousness of love. They're marvelous healers. Doctors, surgeons, and others are amazed at the wonderful healings performed by these individuals through the consciousness of love.

These miracle workers contemplate the wonders of the Infinite Intelligence that guides the planets and causes the sun to shine. They realize the indescribable beauty of God, the absolute harmony in nature, and the Divine love that flows through everyone, including the mother trying to heal her child of infantile paralysis, and the soldier who gives his life in battle to save his comrades. People with that consciousness of love—who understand that the will of God for everyone is life, love, truth, and beauty—are the greatest healers.

⊶✝⊷

Dr. Helen Flanders Dunbar, a distinguished psychiatrist who also earned degrees in theology, wrote a book called *Emotions and Bodily Changes: A Survey of Literature on Psychosomatic Interrelationships*. In this work, she describes a case in which a woman began to lose her sight after her sister was taken to a psychiatric institution. The woman felt guilty because she believed that she hadn't been kind to her sister, and she wanted to punish herself. She said, "I didn't treat my sister right. I should have been nicer and more understanding," and so on. When the doctors told her that it wasn't her fault that her sister had been admitted to a psychiatric hospital, she regained her inner peace and her vision cleared up perfectly. She realized what she was doing to herself and that she had to forgive herself and her sister.

Dr. Dunbar also writes that the skin—more than any other part of the body—reflects the relationship of people's thoughts, feelings, and emotions to their health. Dr. Dunbar brings out the great truth that the skin is the place where the inner world communicates with the external world. She notes that skin conditions are usually caused by repressed emotions, anger, or self-condemnation.

Some years ago, a surgeon friend of mine was suffering from ulcers in his right hand. As we were talking one day, he said, "You know, this hand of mine won't heal. I've tried everything under the sun. I've gone to specialists, I've used ointments and lotions, and I've tried all kinds therapy, yet these ulcers won't go away."

I asked him, "Did you do something you feel guilty about?"

"Yes," he said, and blushed, "but that was years ago when I was an intern."

"Would you do it now?" I continued.

"No, I wouldn't," he replied.

"Well," I said, "you're condemning an innocent man. You're not the same person you were then. Mentally you're different, for you have a new vision of life. Physically you're not the same because every 11 months we create a new body, including our bones. And spiritually you're certainly not the person you used to be. You're therefore harshly judging an innocent soul.

"The God Presence doesn't condemn—Its tendency is to heal. If you cut yourself, It heals you; if you burn yourself, It reduces the edema and creates new skin and tissue. The will of God for everyone is life, love, truth, and beauty . . . something transcending your fondest dreams. The tendency of life is to heal and restore—even the psychotic or the raving maniac. Life wants to return that person to harmony, health, and peace. That's the movement, rhythm, and way of the Divine Presence. God is the Life Principle animating all people. It can't be sick or frustrated. It wants to express Itself through you as order, beauty, and well-being. But you're condemning yourself, and as long as you do that, you can't be healed. Your self-condemnation is blocking the healing. It's just the same as if the pipe in your sink were stopped up with debris, corrosion, and rust. The water is waiting to come through, but it can't."

My explanation was the cure. In a week's time, the doctor's ulcers healed and he was able to perform surgeries again. In addition, he was able to resume playing his violin, which he loved to do. His self-condemnation and feelings of guilt had prevented his hand from healing for two years, but now he was completely healthy.

When you feel guilty, you believe that you must be punished, and then you experience fear and the inability to heal. All of this is caused by false belief. The authors of the Bible understood these truths thousands of years ago. They wrote: "As a man thinks in his heart, so is he." The heart is your subconscious mind and the seat of emotions. There are many buried thoughts in your mind that have a life of their own. These subconscious beliefs and assumptions dictate and control all of your conscious actions and greatly influence your health.

Alcoholics can't be healed if they won't let go of their self-criticism, guilt, and hatred for themselves and others. They must give up all of these things and have goodwill in their hearts for everyone, for love is the fulfillment of the law of health and harmony. They must pour out love and peace and wish for every living being in the world what they desire for themselves. They always know when they've forgiven someone because they can meet that person in their mind and feel no sting of resentment. Instead, they experience a wave of well-being and bliss.

Spiritual healing is real. Turn to the miraculous Healing Presence within you and realize that It's now expressing Itself through you as wholeness, beauty, and perfection. As you fill your mind with these truths of God, and as you forgive everybody—including yourself—you'll experience marvelous healings. For example, Father Jameson, an Episcopal priest, was diagnosed with cancer. His surgeon told him that it had metastasized throughout his body. Father Jameson asked the members of his congregation to pray for him, and he also prayed for himself. He did radiation therapy and suffered excruciating pain, but eventually the surgeon told him that the cancer was disappearing. The priest experienced a complete healing, and five years later, he's perfectly healthy. He believed that the Almighty Power that made his body could heal him, and he was restored.

If you cling to ignorance, superstition, fear, and the belief that God wills you to suffer, you won't heal. That's blindness! Realize that it's normal and natural for you to be healthy, happy, joyous, and free. Know that your body is an instrument in which God dwells and that you're the tabernacle of the Living God. The Healing Presence is within you, and wonders can happen in your life as you begin to turn to It. *Great peace have they who love thy law. And nothing shall offend them. With mine eyes stayed on thee, there is no evil on my pathway.*

The Divine God is always within you. Realize now that the miraculous Healing Power shatters all problems and allows the Healing Power of God to flow through you.

Millions of people are psychologically and spiritually blind because they don't know that they become what they think about all day long. They don't realize that when they're hateful, resentful, or envious of others, they're actually secreting mental poisons that tend to destroy them. That's their disease. All sickness is caused by a lack of peace and ill will. They're constantly thinking that there's no way to solve their problems and that their situation is hopeless. They're saying, "God can't heal me."

Such an attitude is the result of spiritual blindness. You'll only begin to see clearly when you get a new understanding of your mental powers and develop a conscious awareness that the wisdom and intelligence in your subconscious can solve all your problems. Yes, the Healing Power of God is within you, and wonders will happen in your life as you begin to say, "God in the midst of me is healing me now."

Everyone should become aware of the relationship between the conscious and subconscious mind. After careful introspection, people who were once blind to the eternal truths will begin to see that health, wealth, happiness, and peace of mind can be theirs through the correct application of the laws of mind and the way of the spirit.

⁃⊹⊹⁃

There's only One Universal Healing Principle operating through everything. It's in the dog, the cat, the tree, the bird, and the soil. It's the life of all things. There are many ways to use Divine Power, but they all rely on having faith. *According to your faith, it is done unto you.* This law is always in operation whether you're aware of it or not. However, it's far better to know that you're using the law and how you're applying it.

⁃⊹⊹⁃

Spiritual treatment means that you turn to the indwelling God and remind yourself of Infinite Spirit's peace, harmony, wholeness, beauty, boundless love, and limitless power. Know that God loves and cares for you. As you pray this way, your fears will gradually fade away. *All things are possible to him that believeth.*

If you pray about a heart condition, don't think of the organ as diseased, for thoughts are things. Your spiritual thought takes the form of cells, tissue, nerves, and organs. Therefore, focusing on a damaged heart or high blood pressure tends to create more of the same problem. Cease dwelling on symptoms, disease, or any part of the body. Turn your mind to God and His love. Feel and know that there's only One Healing Presence and Power and that nothing can block the action of Infinite Intelligence. Lovingly affirm that the uplifting, strengthening power of the

Infinite Healing Presence is flowing through you now, making you whole. Know and feel that the Almighty Power manifests in you as strength, peace, vitality, wholeness, and right action. Get a clear realization of this, and the damaged heart or other diseased organs will be cured in the light of God's love. God, in the midst of you, is healing you now. Glorify Him in your body now and forevermore.

In a Nutshell

There's only One Healing Power, although it goes by many names, such as God, Infinite Healing Presence, Divine Love, Providence, Nature, or the Life Principle.

We're all natural healers for the simple reason that the Healing Presence of God is within every human. We can all contact It with our thoughts, and It responds to everyone.

There are three steps in the healing process. The first is not to be afraid of the condition that ails you. The second is to realize that illness is only the product of past thinking, which will have no more power as you continue to do affirmative prayer treatment. The third step is to mentally exalt the miraculous Healing Power of God within you.

It's no use petitioning God and begging for healing. God doesn't respond to beseeching or supplication, but to your belief, conviction, and understanding.

Spiritual healing is real. It's the Healing Power within that made you. Turn to the Divine Source and realize that It's now expressing Itself through you as wholeness, beauty, and perfection. As you fill your mind with these truths of God and forgive everybody—including yourself—you'll experience marvelous healings.

Turn your mind to God and His love. Feel and know that there's only One Healing Presence and Power. Realize that the

Infinite Intelligence manifests in you as strength, peace, vitality, wholeness, and right action. Get a clear realization of this, and all disease will be cured in the light of God's love. God in the midst of you is healing you now.

$$Chapter\ Three$$

"All the World Believes a Lie"

"All the world believes a lie, so when I tell it the truth, it thinks I'm telling a lie," stated Phineas Parkhurst Quimby. Quimby was one of America's greatest healers, and this was one of his favorite statements.

What's the lie? Well, the great fabrication, of course, is that external things are causative. Now, the scientific thinker won't give power to the world of phenomena, which is an effect rather than a cause. No, the rational thinker gives power to the *Creator*, not to the created thing. As we're told in the Bible: "Hear, O Israel: The Lord our God, the Lord is one." There's *One* Power—not two, three, or a thousand. The Infinite Presence and Power is within you, and therefore, you're not subject to forces outside yourself.

Some people think that the night air can give them a cold or pneumonia. Nonsense! The night air consists of oxygen, nitrogen, helium, and a few other gases. It's completely innocuous. The night air never said, "I'll give you a chill or the sniffles." Then there are individuals who believe that if their feet get wet, they'll catch a cold. That's ridiculous! Water is harmless. It can't make you sick, and you shouldn't attribute any influence to it. Men, women, children, the sun, the moon, and the stars are also created things; and you shouldn't give power to them either.

The truth is as the Bible says: "As a man thinks in his heart, so is he." Your thoughts and feelings create your destiny. Your heart is your subconscious, and whatever you impress on it comes forth as form, experiences, and events.

⇥✦⇤

Shakespeare wrote: "There is nothing good or bad, but thinking makes it so." That's an absolute truth. Some people say, "Strawberries give me hives." Well, if that were true, everybody in the world who ate strawberries would get hives . . . but they don't! Individuals who have such an allergic reaction have made a law for themselves and have a bad relationship with strawberries. When they say, "Strawberries give me hives," that's a command to their subconscious. Then when they eat this fruit, the subconscious sees the strawberries coming and says, "The boss wants hives." And the deeper mind proceeds to give them an allergy attack.

This is the kind of law that people make for themselves. You might say, "I can't eat mushrooms because they give me acute indigestion." That's a law you made for yourself. Millions of people eat mushrooms without getting sick. If it were a law, everybody in the world would suffer accordingly.

Similarly, some people say that ragweed gives them asthma or hay fever. If that were a cosmic law, everybody on the planet who came into contact with these plants would begin to tear up and have an allergy attack. This is equivalent to a woman saying, "I'm allergic to red roses." If you hypnotize her, put a glass of distilled water under her nose, and say, "This is a red rose," she'll develop all the symptoms right there in front of you. Where's the allergy? Isn't it in her own mind? It surely isn't in the distilled water! Ragweed is the same substance as your own bloodstream, for there's only One Substance. God is the only Presence, Power, and Cause.

Everything is Spirit made manifest, including strawberries and mushrooms. Everything is God.

Don't judge according to appearances. The five senses provide an avalanche of data, but you don't have to become a victim of your sensory perceptions. You can reject what you see or hear. You can see peace instead of discord, love instead of hatred, joy instead of sadness, and light instead of darkness. You can discipline your senses and taste the sweet truth of God.

I visited Dr. Viktor Frankl, a distinguished psychiatrist, some years ago. During World War II, the Nazis imprisoned him in Auschwitz and murdered his wife and parents. Frankl survived the atrocities, and after the war he wrote a book called *Man's Search for Meaning,* which describes his experiences in the concentration camp and how he found a reason to live in the midst of unspeakable brutality. He also discusses his belief that life always has meaning, even in the most difficult of circumstances.

Frankl noted that he and the other doctors with whom he was imprisoned learned that many of the assumptions they had about the human body were false. For example, they had to take cold showers and stand in the chilly air with no clothes on; they weren't even given a towel to dry themselves. It was late autumn and the weather was very cold, but they didn't get sick. Frankl said, "We were surprised that we didn't catch cold. The medical men among us learned first of all that the textbooks tell lies."

Frankl also discussed how surprised he was by how much he and the other prisoners could endure. He said, "We slept in beds that were constructed in tiers. On each tier, measuring about six to eight feet, nine men slept directly on the hard boards, sharing only two blankets. We could lie only on our sides, crowded and huddled against each other. Although it was forbidden to take shoes up to the bunks, some people did use them secretly as pillows in spite of the fact that they were caked with mud."

Frankl continued, "Now, I would like to mention another surprise about how much we could endure. We were unable to clean our teeth, yet in spite of that and a severe vitamin deficiency, we had healthier gums than ever before."

The ways of the Infinite are beyond our understanding. Frankl and some of the other prisoners should have developed pneumonia, but they didn't because they were dwelling in a higher level of consciousness.

Dr. Fleet of London told me that during the war, she and many other people could only find starchy foods to eat. They couldn't have the meats, fruits, and vegetables they were accustomed to. She said that despite the deprivation and pressure of war, they stayed calm and tried to help people. "We had no vitamins, and our diet was contrary to the science of nutrition, but we were healthier than before," Dr. Fleet stated. As this doctor found out, we don't have to become victims of the beliefs of the mass mind circulating in the world.

Not many people know that Virginia Graham's success in her famous TV show *Girl Talk* came after she'd conquered a diagnosis of terminal cancer and made medical history. Virginia's doctor described the miracle that Virginia experienced in these words: "She purified her bloodstream with her thoughts." Virginia prayed fervently and knew that she'd be healed and would live. "I have a surviving point of view," she said. Her love of life was clear—and was probably one of the reasons her TV show climbed to the top of the ratings.

A psychologist described a student of his who had clairvoyant vision: She saw a plane on fire in a field. This student and another woman went and prayed in that area. They contemplated love, peace, harmony, beauty, and right action in their minds and hearts. They immersed themselves in the Holy Omnipresence. And then they saw a plane coming out of the clouds in flames. It cracked and fell to the ground.

Although in the student's vision, the two men on the plane had burned to death, she now saw that they were completely unharmed, even though the plane had been destroyed.

One of the men said, "I was about to throw myself out of the plane but suddenly experienced a sense of absolute peace and safety, and I sat back down." Clearly, in the higher levels of your mind, you can't be burned—these women proved that, and it's absolutely true.

Phineas Parkhurst Quimby stated years ago that sickness is caused by the mind. He also said that people often get their infections in the church. They develop a guilt complex and fear there that makes them ill. They form a belief in a punitive God and came to think that He's punishing them. Quimby had to teach them that God is a loving Presence.

Quimby said that if you tell people who've never heard of cancer that they have the disease, it has no effect whatsoever upon them. But if you tell those who've heard all about the ravages of cancer that they have a malignancy, they may fall down in terror, and that fearful state may itself cause a cancer to develop.

⊰✦⊱

Lao-tzu said that when a sage goes forth into the jungle, he carries no sword or spear. He isn't afraid of a javelin or a rhinoceros because there's no place in him that can be wounded. In other words, he's built up immunity and received the Divine antibody.

⊰✦⊱

You're frequently deceived by what you look at. For example, a stick inserted in water appears to be broken, and when you stand on a railroad track, the two parallel lines of the rails seem to come together in the distance. Your eyes can trick you because they only deal with surface appearances. People say the sun rises and sets. Actually, it does neither. We see nothing as it is in reality because our eyes are geared to see according to our beliefs. If our minds were conditioned in any other way, we'd see things differently. A piece of steel seems solid, but x-rays reveal it to be porous—just like our bodies. In reality, everything is made up of trillions of microscopic particles in perpetual motion.

⊰✦⊱

If you say that you believe that the configuration of the stars in the sky determines your fate, you're making an external thing a cause and are jinxing yourself. The stars have no power over you—your beliefs do. Let's say that your sister and you are identical twins and, of course, were born under the same stars. She's taken up the study of the Science of Mind or a similar philosophy and is leading a marvelous and wonderful life. You, on the other hand, are suffering from your belief in an ominous configuration of the stars, and everything is going wrong for you. Your problems are caused by your beliefs. Whatever you believe, your subconscious manifests it. So it's extremely dangerous to think that the planets or the stars are working against you.

Too many people believe this lie. However, when they're told the truth, they still refuse to believe it. They think that God is up there punishing them. The truth is that the Life Principle can't punish you; It forgives you. If you burn yourself, It forgives you and gives you new skin and tissue. If you cut yourself, It repairs the wound. It's always seeking to heal. The Infinite can't punish you because Its eyes are too pure to behold iniquity.

God is the eternal now, and now is the moment of salvation. You're not a victim of karma or the past because you're dealing with a timeless, spaceless Presence. Therefore, there's no past to worry about. Nothing matters but this moment. Change this moment, and you transform your destiny. A new beginning is a new end. You create a fresh start when you enthrone godlike ideas in your mind and live with them. Then the desert of your life will rejoice and blossom like a rose. That's the good news, the gospel, and the truth of being. You can change your mind now.

⊰✝⊱

When you "emotionalize" thoughts and accept them as true, they sink into your subconscious and manifest themselves in your body and affairs. For example, Gary L. believed a lie. He was gradually going blind. The ophthalmologist couldn't find anything radically wrong with his eyes, but Gary consulted an astrologist who told him the problem was in his planetary birth chart. The real cause of his eye trouble, however, was that he hated his wife because he thought she nagged him. The trouble was within himself. He frequently said, "I hate the sight of my wife," "I can't stand to look at her," and "I can't see my way out this situation because I have two children and they need her."

His subconscious accepted these feelings and statements and responded by occluding his vision. It had nothing to do with the alignment of the planets or the stars.

I arranged for Gary and his wife to meet with me, and I explained the workings of the mind. She cooperated by ceasing to nag. They began to pray together, seeing God in each other. They also started speaking to one another kindly and lovingly. Moreover, every morning and evening they spent time together reading psalms and other spiritual writings.

In a month's time, Gary's vision was back to normal, and the ophthalmologist congratulated him. Gary had been lying to himself by blaming the stars and planets when the true cause was his destructive, negative emotions.

Many people think that disease is "out there" and that the body can catch it. That's one of the lies the world believes. In fact, all disease is of the mind. Nothing happens in the body unless it first happens in the mind. To illustrate, Andrew L. had been suffering from colitis for a long time when he came to see me. He'd been taking medicine, resting, and following a special diet. However, he was lying to himself, blaming heredity and diet for causing his illness. He said, "Colitis runs in my family. My grandmother and mom had it. I'm sure the food I eat also has something to do with my trouble."

I described to Andrew a study conducted by Dr. Helen Flanders Dunbar on a group of colitis patients in New York. Her research showed that in a number of cases, the men who suffered from colitis were too emotionally tied to their mothers and had never been away from them for more than 30 days in their entire lives.

None of these men was married, and the onset of their colitis was associated with a conflict between the mother tie and the men's desire for marriage.

Andrew had a similar conflict: His mother had dominated him all of his life, and he was afraid to defy her. He felt guilty if he didn't obey her wishes and took the commandment "Honor thy father and mother" literally.

I explained to him that the commandment doesn't mean that we have to do exactly what our parents want. I told him to pray for his mom and wish only the best for her, and she'd come to the realization that she was preventing him from experiencing true happiness.

A few months later, Andrew came to see me again. He told me that his mother had changed and that their relationship had improved. He'd met a fine young lady and told his mom that he planned to marry her. She accepted his decision and welcomed the woman into the family.

Andrew's colitis cleared up "miraculously" in a few weeks. He'd been deceiving himself for several years, failing to see that the cause of his sickness was purely emotional—provoked by the poisonous pocket of resentment in the crevices of his soul. He didn't deliberately give himself colitis; his trouble was caused by the accumulation of his negative and destructive thoughts.

-§✝§-

The subconscious mind is a law. It arranges all deposited thoughts into complex patterns. These patterns are not only the cause of all ills, but also the source of our successes and triumphs. The great lie is the belief in material causation. We blame conditions, the environment, circumstances, and sometimes God for our problems, but all difficulties are caused by mental patterns and beliefs lodged in our subconscious mind. For instance, Annie K. was very upset about her aunt. She told me that her aunt was kindhearted, religious, and generous, but now was suffering from a devastating heart condition. Annie asked why God didn't do something to help her aunt. I hear this question from so many people. It exemplifies one of the great misunderstandings we have about God. Both Annie and her aunt were completely deceived in believing that sickness is independent of the mind. That's the great lie that the world believes—that illness is "out there" and that they can "catch" it.

Belief in this fallacy will prevent recovery. Annie's aunt had a coronary condition that she believed was incurable. Her father had died from a similar condition, and she was certain that she would, too. So, naturally she wasn't healing. However, once she accepted that she was laboring under a false belief, she made excellent progress. She ceased to believe the lie that her heart was a material object with laws of its own. She now believes that her body is subject to her thoughts and feelings. As she changes her mind, she transforms her body. She prays regularly and systematically, knowing that Divine Presence is flowing through her as beauty, wholeness, vitality, and strength and that God's love dwells in her mind and body. She realized that sickness has no power beyond that which she gives it in her own mind, and she experienced a complete healing.

⛧

When trouble of any kind comes, look upon it as nature's signal that your thinking has gone astray, and then change your thoughts. All of your experiences are the result of your subconscious beliefs and assumptions. No matter what happens in your life, it's simply an outpouring of your subconscious mind. Every condition, event, and circumstance that you experience is the result of your subconscious patterns—your beliefs and conditioning.

Moreover, we all have many beliefs and ideas that we've long since forgotten—perhaps going back to childhood—hidden in the deeper recesses of our subconscious. They have the power to influence our lives. For example, if you were taught that sitting near a fan will give you a stiff neck, your subconscious mind will see to it that when you do sit near a fan, your neck suffers. The problem isn't the fan, which is made up of innocuous molecules of energy oscillating at a high frequency, but your erroneous beliefs. I've seen people working under a fan all day, and it has no effect whatsoever upon them. The fan itself is harmless.

When Jack M. came to see me, he was extremely upset. Earlier that day, he'd had a bad accident that totaled both his car and the automobile of the other driver. The other driver was hurt, and Jack had barely escaped serious injury. He wondered what he'd done to deserve such trouble. He said that he'd sensed that something bad was going to happen. He'd read his horoscope that morning, and it said that there was a great danger of a car accident and that he should be careful. Jack said that he was filled with fear when he read it. He didn't want to drive that day, but he had to go for a job interview.

His great fear brought on the accident, for thoughts that are "emotionalized" are manifested by the subconscious. His deeper mind took his anxiety as a request and created it on the screen of space. What you sow, you shall surely reap. There's only One Power: the Spirit within you. There's no other power, cause, or substance in the universe. The planets and stars are all just molecules moving in space, and they have nothing to do with your life.

I gave Jack a prayer to use regularly, telling him that if he filled his mind with these great truths, his subconscious mind would accept them accordingly, and he'd be compelled to drive harmoniously and safely:

My car is God's idea. It moves from point to point freely, joyously, and lovingly. God's wisdom guides this car in all its ways. God's order, symmetry, and beauty govern the mechanism of this car at all times. God's Holy Presence blesses this car and all its occupants. As the driver, I am an ambassador of God. I am full of love and goodwill for everyone. God's peace, truth, and understanding always govern me. God directs all of my decisions, making my way straight, beautiful, and perfect. The Spirit of the Lord is upon me, making all roads a highway for God.

⚜✠⚜

In order for your world to change, you have to change your mind—you can't go on thinking the same old way. To think in a new way, you have to get some new ideas and learn about the laws of mind. Realize that your thoughts are creative. Whatever you impress on the subconscious—whether it's good or bad—is expressed. Therefore, begin to have a healthy respect for your thoughts.

Many people blame the weather for their colds, aches, pains, and depression. They also blame others, saying things like, "That man at work is blocking my good. If it weren't for him, I'd get promoted." When you do this, you're making a god of another person. That's a big lie. There's only *One* God. The Bible says: "You shall not make for yourself an idol in the form of anything in heaven above or on the earth beneath or in the waters below. You shall not bow down to them or worship them; for I, the Lord your God, am a jealous God."

This passage means that you shouldn't give any power to external events or other people, for there's only One Power. Don't put another person on a pedestal and say, "You're a new God I have to worship."

There's only One Being. It's the Infinite Presence and Power within you. It's omnipotent, and nothing can oppose it. It created the world. It's the all-powerful Eternal One. Say to yourself: "I want good health. Infinite Spirit opens up a new opportunity that allows me to express myself at the highest level and be free from illness and full of vitality." Go to the Source and realize that the power of the Almighty backs you up.

Stop believing in the big lie. Stop polluting the atmosphere with strange notions, false doctrines, and weird beliefs. People complain about environmental pollution, but you never hear them talk about the pollution of the mind, which includes resentment, hostility, and hate. You must learn the great truth that no person, situation, or condition causes you to be ill, unhappy, or lonesome. There's no one to blame.

If someone calls you a jerk, are you going to get angry and upset? Just say, "You have no power to upset me today; God's peace fills your soul" or "God loves me and cares for me," and go on about your business.

Now, don't tell me that that person has the power to bother you. If you do, you're suffering from the biggest lie of all time. The suggestions and statements of others have no real power to hurt you.

It's the movement of your own mind that determines how you feel, and there's no law preventing you from saying, "God loves and cares for me." You can thereby neutralize negative or angry thoughts.

⛨

Some people blame the devil for their problems, but no such being exists. There's only *One* Power; there can't be two, three, or a thousand. That's the greatest of all truths. *Devil* spelled backward is *lived*. If you're living life backwards, that's your evil or devil, isn't it? When you deviate from the truth or misuse the law, you see through a glass darkly. Therefore, misunderstanding is the only devil there is.

⚜

One time a banker told me that several members of his staff were out sick with the flu. He was afraid of catching it, too, and wanted to know how to protect himself. I advised him to completely reject the idea of infection because it really had no power over him unless he gave it credence. I told him to stop telling himself that he was vulnerable to the virus because thoughts are powerful, and nothing manifest in our lives except through the creative power of the mind. He affirmed frequently as follows:

> *The Father and I are one. I live now and have my being in the Healing Presence. God lives, moves, and has His being in me. God cannot get sick. The Spirit is never hurt or wounded. What is true of God is true of me, and therefore, I cannot be sick. I am perfect health. God is my health. Health is mine. Joy is mine. Peace is mine. I feel wonderful.*

You can rest assured that he didn't get the flu.

⚜

You're in charge of your own mind, and you have the wonderful opportunity to affirm that God's peace and love fill your heart, mind, and entire being. The Power is always in you. When you say, "I am," you're announcing the Presence and the Power of God in yourself. It's Pure Being and Life Awareness. It's the One Presence, Power, Cause, and Substance. *The Lord is my light and my salvation. Whom shall I fear? The Lord is the strength of my life. Of whom shall I be afraid?*

The Lord is your own consciousness, awareness, and Life Principle. God, in the midst of you, is guiding you now. His peace fills your soul and His love saturates your entire being. *"I will restore health to you and heal you of your wounds,"* says the Lord.

In a Nutshell

The great lie is the belief in material causation. We blame conditions, the environment, circumstances, and sometimes God, but all difficulties are caused by mental patterns and beliefs lodged in our subconscious mind.

The Life Principle can't punish you; It always forgives you. If you burn yourself, It forgives you and gives you new skin and tissue. It's always seeking to heal.

The subconscious mind is a law. It arranges all deposited thoughts into complex patterns that are the cause of both your ills and your triumphs.

In order for your world to change, you have to change your mind. You can't go on thinking the same old way—you have to get some new ideas.

Whatever you impress on the subconscious—whether it's good or bad—manifests in your life. Therefore, begin to have a healthy respect for your thoughts.

There's no past to worry about—the past is dead. Nothing matters but this moment. Change this moment and you'll transform your destiny.

⛨ ⛨

Chapter Four

How to Use Your Healing Power

*A*ll over the world men and women of various creeds are developing a growing understanding of the application of mental and spiritual laws in the fields of medicine, psychiatry, psychology, and other related areas. Many articles are being published describing how destructive mental and emotional conflicts can cause all kinds of disease. One of the pioneering books in this field is Dr. Helen Flanders Dunbar's *Emotions and Bodily Changes*, a magnificent work on the mental and emotional causes of various maladies.

This increasing interest in the law of the mind is a sign that the reign of the five senses—the belief in material causation—is coming to an end. In its place, belief in Divine Intelligence and the Infinite Healing Presence in all things is being reestablished. *Bless the Lord, O my soul . . . Who heals all your diseases, Who Redeems your life from destruction, Who crowns you with lovingkindness and tender mercies, Who satisfies your mouth with good things, so that your youth is renewed like the eagle's.*

The Bible is a psychological textbook that teaches us how to overcome all problems. It explains how we get into trouble and how to get out of it. It teaches the science of life and the meaning of symbols. When I write or speak about the wonderful biblical stories, I ask my Higher Self: *What did the writers of these stories mean when they wrote them?* And the mind that wrote them is the mind that reads them, for there's only one mind common to all individuals.

You can become quiet and feel the Infinite Intelligence within you, revealing everything you need to know. Your consciousness contains the memory of everything that's ever transpired, and it's possible for you to tune in to that vast ocean of wisdom within you. The same Healing Presence that Moses, Paul, and Jesus used is available today. It's the Living Spirit that created you. Use this Presence and Power, go forward in the light, and move from glory to glory until the dawn appears and all shadows flee.

The Bible says: "The Spirit of the Lord God is upon me, because the Lord has anointed me to preach good tidings to the poor. He has sent me to heal the brokenhearted, to proclaim liberty to the captives, and the opening of the prison to those who are bound."

The Spirit of the Lord is upon you right now, and your good is in this moment—not tomorrow, next week, or next year, but this minute. *Now* is the day of salvation, so why wait for a healing? Why say, "Someday I'll have peace"? The peace of God is within you in this moment. You can claim: "God's river of peace flows through me right now, saturating my mind, heart, and entire being." No matter what you're seeking, it exists now.

Why wait to have power? The power of the Almighty is already within you, and you'll receive energy and strength as you call upon It. It always answers you. Love is here in this very moment, and you can experience Divine compassion welling up in your heart for all people. You can say, "God's love floods my mind, heart, and being." And the God of love will respond. *Call upon me; I will answer you.*

You can also attract your Divine companion now. What you're seeking for the future is present now . . . right where you are. The nature of the Infinite Presence and Power is to respond to you. *When you call upon Him, He answers you. He will be with you in trouble, and He will set you on High because you have known His name.*

Someone asked me in one of my classes if the stories of healing in the Bible are true. The answer is simple: The Healing Principle is eternal and has always been available to all people everywhere. The Healing Presence is omnipresent—it's in the dog, the cat, the tree, the soil, and everything else. It's therefore within you, too. It created you from a cell and knows all the processes and functions of your body. It's all-wise and all-knowing.

In order to understand the Bible, see it as a great psychological drama taking place in the consciousness of all people throughout the world. Look upon the stories recorded in the Bible as allegories about yourself and your friends awakening from darkness to the light within.

God is the savior within and knows the solutions to all problems. He knows and sees everything. Look upon God as yourself, filled with faith and confidence. Reject all false beliefs and ideas and announce the presence of your ideal.

In ancient times, it was believed that people who were insane were possessed by demons or devils. Exorcism in its various forms became the accepted treatment for these individuals. Exorcists would use holy water and the Bible and pronounce the name of *God* to compel the demons to flee.

In fact, the "evil spirits" were dark emotions, such as hatred, resentment, jealousy, revenge, fear, and so on. In modern times, psychiatrists, psychologists, and spiritual leaders try to help people suffering from mental disorders cleanse their mind of all negative thoughts and false beliefs.

A young man who was traveling on an ocean liner to India saw a raving maniac completely healed by an American woman who prayed aloud for him. He had a remarkable, instantaneous healing. Being curious, the young man asked the woman what she'd done. She replied, "I claimed that God's love and peace filled his mind and entire being and that God was right there." Her realization of the Presence and Power in the afflicted man was instantaneously resurrected in his mind, and a healing followed. Her faith made him whole.

All demons and devils are negative states of mind, for there's only one God—not two, three, or a thousand. There's One Presence who lives in the hearts of all people. That's why the greatest truth is the biblical injunction: "Hear, O Israel: The Lord our God, the Lord is one."

The Bible says that we must go into our own synagogue. *Synagogue* in the Bible refers to the temple of our mind. Through spiritual awareness, we cast out of our consciousness all false theories, dogmas, and beliefs—as well as negative states such as resentment, ill will, hatred, and jealousy. These are the real devils. Obsessions, dual personalities, and all other mental aberrations are the result of habitual negative thinking that has crystallized into a definite state of mind.

If you're praying for a mentally ill person, follow the teachings of the Bible. Go into your synagogue and rehearse in your mind the truths of God. Feel the mental atmosphere of freedom and peace for the sick person. Be full of faith and confidence, giving no power to symptoms or mental blocks. Completely reject the negative prognoses and opinions of those around you. Do this emphatically and with a sense of inner knowing. Know that you have the authority to say the truth, for the Infinite Presence and Power is speaking through you.

By affirming your unity and oneness with God, you're empowered to cast out demons. Silently or audibly, speak the words of health, harmony, and inner peace with feeling and faith. Pray with confidence, and the spell of evil thoughts will be broken. Once and for all, completely reject the power of any so-called negative or evil forces. Don't admit for one moment that demons have any power or that there even are such entities.

Phineas Parkhurst Quimby, the great American healer, knew that when he thought about his patients, he was in command of their mind and body. Therefore, he contemplated their Divine perfection and duplicated many of the miracles recorded in the Bible. Quimby's inner conviction was that what was true of God was true of his patients. He declared the truth and healed them.

Doctors and scientists are conducting experiments in hypnosis. They've learned that they can cause a subject under hypnosis to act like an insane person through the power of suggestion. For instance, people under hypnosis who are told to jump with one foot in the air when they see a dog will do so. If the suggestion isn't removed, they'll continue to jump whenever a dog appears—even after being awakened from the trance. This is called *compulsion*.

Similarly, you can be told that a bad spirit or the devil possesses you, and your subconscious mind, which acts upon suggestion, faithfully embraces the idea, compelling you to act as though you were haunted.

Many people write me that they hear voices all the time, telling them terrible things. They believe that evil spirits possess them. I tell them that I also hear voices and that clairaudience is a faculty of the human mind. It's the Intelligence within us that enables our objective mind to receive communications from our subconscious. In fact, a few weeks ago I clearly heard an answer to a question that had perplexed me for some time. The words didn't come from some outside entity but from my own deeper mind, which is one with Infinite Intelligence.

Needless to say, the law of mind governs the character of clairaudient manifestations. For example, if you believe that a guardian angel is speaking to you, your subconscious will follow the suggestion given and assume the guise of an angel.

The subconscious mind possesses transcendent powers and can be influenced negatively or positively. Be sure that you only feed it constructive, harmonious thoughts. You must not place gangsters, assassins, and murderers in charge of your mind. Instead, let wisdom and Divine love lead you. Allow your faith in God and all things good direct your mind.

Contemplate the Infinite perfection within you and keep on doing so until the day breaks and the shadows flee. As you dwell in the secret place and contemplate God in His glory within you, you'll abide in the shadow of the Almighty and know that His love surrounds and enfolds you, making your way straight, beautiful, and joyous.

⊣✦⊢

The Divine Intelligence is sovereign and supreme. It responds to your thoughts and is your refuge and fortress. The Infinite Presence inspires, strengthens, and restores your mind and body. It's beneficent and kind. Trust It completely, for It responds as mercy, love, inspiration, and indescribable beauty. It's the wonderful healing Power. *"I will restore health to you and heal you of your wounds,"* *says the Lord.*

⊣✦⊢

When you focus your attention on the idea of perfect health, the Almighty Power will flow through your focal point of attention, and a healing will follow. This is exemplified in the story from the Bible in which Jesus heals a leper: "And behold, a leper came to him and knelt before him, saying, 'Lord, if you will, you can make me clean.' And Jesus stretched out his hand and touched him, saying, 'I will; be clean.' And immediately his leprosy was cleansed."

Biblically speaking, a leper is someone who, through erroneous thoughts, has become separated from the Divine Source of mind and life. A leper is a person who's governed by the five senses and filled with fears, superstitions, and unsound beliefs.

You can cleanse yourself by forgiving everyone and wishing for them all the blessings of life, including peace, love, joy, and happiness. Also forgive *yourself* for harboring negative thoughts.

You live in the love, the light, and the glory of God. Having cleansed your mind of all impurities, negative imagery, and destructive thoughts, become absorbed in the joy of experiencing an answered prayer. This consumes the old state and gives birth to the new.

You've probably seen or heard about men and women laying hands on people to heal them. I saw a healer in England place his hands on individuals suffering from arthritis or other problems, and they were healed. Sometimes those who practice the laying on of hands are called *natural healers,* but actually we're *all* natural healers for the simple reason that the Infinite Healing Presence is within everyone. We can contact It with our thoughts, and It responds to everyone. It's omnipresent and is the very life of all things.

Nothing is too big or little to be healed. Some people have healed their ulcers through faith, while others have overcome what appeared to be incurable malignancies. It's just as easy for the Infinite Presence to regenerate a cancerous pancreas as a scraped knee, for the Almighty Intelligence is omnipotent and all-wise. It's the Power that guides the planets and causes the Earth to revolve on its axis.

It's wise to refrain from going around telling everyone that you've had a spiritual healing. Many of your friends will make derogatory and skeptical remarks, which might undermine your faith, cause you to doubt, and undo the benefits you've received from prayer.

If you want a healing in your body, withdraw mentally from the symptoms and evidence of the senses. Begin to think of the Infinite Healing Presence within you, focusing on health, harmony, and peace. Put all of your attention on well-being and peace of mind. The Almighty Creative Power flows through the focal point of attention and touches every atom of your being. Dwelling in conscious communion with the Divine, it's easy to become intoxicated with Spirit and filled with exhilaration. This spiritual awakening builds you up and renews you so that each day brings you more joy. As you continue to pray scientifically, you're lifted up, an outpouring of Spirit takes place, and your entire being is recharged.

⊰✛⊱

Dr. Alexis Carrel, a Nobel Prize winner in physiology, describes the marvelous effects produced by prayer. He cites the case of a cancerous sore that shriveled to a scar before his eyes. He also recounts seeing wounds repair themselves in a few seconds and pathological symptoms disappear in a few hours. These healings of tumors, burns, and so forth were due to nothing more than the release of the Healing Power within each patient.

God is the only Healer and Power. When we call upon this Presence within, claiming that It saturates our mind and body, we receive a corresponding flood of the Healing Power that permeates every cell of our being, healing wounds and making us whole. Our body begins to function harmoniously. Then we know the truth of the biblical passage: "In my flesh I shall see God."

As you claim and affirm your good, your deeper mind—the law—automatically responds to the new mental patterns and imagery, and a healing follows. All you have to do is conform to the law, and results will follow. The moment you realize the God Presence within, you'll get the outcome you seek, for He's the eternal, boundless being. Change your mind now and you'll transform your future.

I came across a story about a man who was afflicted with illness. His legs would become locked so that he couldn't move. He'd panic and be frozen on the spot—even in the middle of a busy street. This condition of constant fear was wearing him down, so he adopted the following procedure.

First, he aligned himself with the Divine Presence. He turned to the Infinite Source within, which created him and knew what to do. He said to himself, "This Healing Presence is omnipresent, omniscient, and omnipotent." He realized that the Healing Presence was saturating every atom of his being and flowing through him as harmony, health, peace, wholeness, beauty, and perfection.

As he gradually filled his mind with these eternal verities, he became reconditioned to health and harmony. As he changed his mind, he transformed his body and healed, for the physical self is a shadow of the mind.

When we think negatively—when we resent, hate, condemn, or fear another person—we're committing a sin. If we think that there's some force that can challenge the One Power, we're also sinning, because then we're mentally dwelling on evil or the belief in another power, thereby attracting all manner of calamity, trouble, and loss. We go astray when we turn away from our goal in life, which should always be peace, harmony, wisdom, and perfect health. In indulging in morbid and destructive thoughts, we limit our happiness and fulfillment.

You're an expression of the Infinite, and your mind is an off-spring of Spirit. With your mind, you choose. If you err in your judgment, you experience the automatic reaction of your subconscious. However, your mind is always forgiving you: The moment you present it with new mental imagery and lovely patterns of thought, it responds accordingly. This is the love of God and the mercy of the Infinite.

If your loved one is sick, open up your mind and let the healing light in. Surrender the person to God and know that he or she is now immersed in the Holy Omnipresence and is radiant, happy, and free. Claim that what's true of God is true of your beloved. As you continue to do this, he or she will rise up from the bed of pain, misery, and suffering and walk the Earth in perfect health, glorifying the Infinite.

Elsie Salmon, a missionary's wife in South Africa, wrote a book called *He Heals Today,* in which she describes a child who had a deformed left hand missing three fingers. After Elsie performed a prayer treatment, the tiny hand began to unfold like a flower in front of the eyes of her church members. Elsie states that there was no doubt in the minds of the observers that a perfect hand was forming.

We must not look upon this story as miraculous or supernatural. We should instead begin to realize that the Creative Power that makes the body can definitely grow a hand, a leg, or an eye. After all, where did the organs of our body come from? If we make an icebox, can't we repair it if it breaks?

Elsie Salmon's faith in the Creative Power caused the malformed hand to rejuvenate itself. She was aware of the reality of what she prayed for and knew that the nature of the Infinite Intelligence is responsiveness. Similarly, if you're sick or dying of cancer, God can heal you, too. *According to thy faith, it is done unto you.*

Release your hidden power and become a channel of the Divine. Then you'll experience the love, light, and glory of the One Who Forever Is. You can do all things through this God Power that strengthens you.

In a Nutshell

There's but one mind common to all people. The same Healing Presence that served Moses, Paul, and Jesus is within you, and you can use It. It created you from a cell and knows all of the processes and functions of your body. It's all-wise and omnipotent.

You can cast out the demons of negativity by affirming your unity and oneness with God. Silently or audibly speak the words of health, harmony, and inner peace with feeling and faith.

The nature of the deeper mind is to respond to your thought. When you focus your attention on the idea of perfect health, the Power of the Almighty will flow through your focal point of attention, and a healing will follow.

Contemplate the Presence and Power that saturates every atom of your being. Then a wave of inner peace will follow, and all will be well. You can eliminate any sickness by dwelling on the omnipresence, harmony, peace, and love of God.

If you want a healing of your body, withdraw mentally from the symptoms and evidence of the senses. Begin to focus on the Infinite Healing Presence within, and you'll feel the response of Spirit flowing through you, touching every atom of your being.

❈ ❈

Chapter Five

Never Lose Faith

*M*any people are sick and unhappy. Moreover, their work is shoddy because their heart isn't in it. Their attitude toward life is all wrong. Their dreams and ambitions have withered because they don't know how to achieve them. Not knowing the laws of mind and how to pray scientifically, they find their wonderful ideas stillborn in their minds and experience frustration and neurosis.

If you look around your office or where you live, you'll see many people stagnating and dying on the vine. They're constantly criticizing themselves even though within everyone is the Living Spirit Almighty. They destroy their ability to accomplish anything by saying, "If I had John's brains or wealth, or Tom's connections, I could advance and be somebody. But I'm just a nobody. I was born on the wrong side of the tracks and must be satisfied with my lot." That's a foolish philosophy of life, but it's the way many people think.

In fact, your creativity and potential are unlimited. Whenever you turn with confidence to the Almighty Power within, knowing that you're guided by this inner light and that you're expressing yourself fully, you'll become a channel for the Divine and will move from glory to glory.

There's no one in the entire world like you, and God needs you where you are—otherwise, you wouldn't be here. Banish fear, doubt, and ill will from your mind, and completely trust the Divine Presence. Affirm with feeling and humility: "I have faith and confidence. I can do all things through the Infinite Power, which strengthens, comforts, and directs me." As you continue to repeat this prayer, you'll perform wonders.

Raise your sights, realizing that you'll always go where your vision is. Picture what you wish to achieve and have faith that Infinite Wisdom will manifest it on the screen of space. You'll be satisfied for a time, and then Divine discontent will stir in you again, causing you to reach for even higher goals.

You can pray for someone who lives thousands of miles away or who's in the hospital. When you do this, simply affirm in your mind and heart that the person is joyous, happy, and well. See him or her as vibrant and bubbling over with enthusiasm. If your thoughts wander, bring them back and refocus on the images of your desire.

If you're praying for people who are sick, don't visualize them in a hospital. If you do, you're denying your affirmation and are reinforcing the idea of disease by dwelling on their symptoms, aches, and pains. Instead, imagine them at home, in perfect health, telling you about the miracle of their healing. See them as vital and smiling, doing what they enjoy.

The Father in heaven is your own thoughts and feelings—your brain and heart. When they're united, your prayer is answered; and you experience peace, harmony, and well-being.

If you're an employer, you may order your workers to do certain jobs, expecting them to obey. After all, you're paying them to conform to your business methods and processes. In the same manner, you're the master of your thoughts—not the serf or slave. Surely you won't permit the gangsters of hate, fear, prejudice, jealousy, or rage to push you around. *You* are in control.

When you begin to discipline your mind, don't allow the doubt, anxiety, or false impressions of the world to intimidate you. You must remember that emotion follows thought and that when you take charge of your thoughts and mental imagery, nothing can bother you. For example, if someone calls you a snake in the grass, the insult can't hurt you unless you allow it to. You can instead affirm: "God's peace fills that person's mind." It also fills your own mind, of course, for you're in control of the movement of your thoughts. You can act from anger, hate, or revenge . . . or from peace, harmony, and goodwill.

Never give others the power to disturb you. If you do, you're putting them on a pedestal and making gods and goddesses out of them. Realize that they have no ability to annoy you because the power is in *you*. The One Presence and Power is omnipotent and supreme. Why, then, should you bow down to false gods?

The moment you're tempted to react negatively, identify immediately with your aim, which is always peace, harmony, wisdom, right action, and achievement. Focus on your ideal right away and you'll be victorious.

You can put your attention on lack, loss, and misfortune . . . or on success, health, and prosperity. Whatever you imagine and feel to be true comes to pass. Therefore, let your mind become the workshop of God, as it should be. For instance, a mother whose son is rather late in arriving home can begin to imagine that he has met with some disaster and envision him hurt at the hospital.

Or she can focus on healing thoughts and the One Power and Presence, knowing that her son is well.

You're here to let your light shine so that others can see your good works and glorify the Father in heaven. You must have faith and complete trust in the boundless love of the Infinite, which seeks only to express Itself through you. Identify yourself mentally and emotionally with the Divine Presence. Feel and know that you're a channel for the manifestation of all of God's attributes and power. Infinite Spirit flows through you as harmony, health, peace, joy, and abundance.

As you repeat these truths frequently, your mind will become imbued with them, and you'll find yourself compelled to bring forth only that which is good, beautiful, and true. You'll become a Divinely ordained person whose sole mission in the world is to follow the orders of the Eternal One.

Whose directions are *you* carrying out? Whatever ideas you focus on will dominate and compel you. Begin now to realize that there's no limit to your possibilities. Feel and believe that the Divine Presence is your silent partner who counsels and directs you. As you do this, your life will become wonderful, satisfying, and constructive.

Prayer is the contemplation of the truths of God from the highest standpoint. When you say, "God loves and cares for me" or "God is guiding me now," you're praying—and you'll receive a response, for the nature of Infinite Intelligence is responsiveness. *Call upon me, and I will answer you. I will be with you in trouble. I will set you on high because you have known my name.* As you align yourself with Divine Wisdom, you'll live a better life than you ever dreamed of and will be radiant, happy, and free. Through the power of the Almighty, you'll accomplish great things.

The Bible describes how Jesus raised a widow's son from the dead:

> And when He came near the gate of the city, behold, a dead man was being carried out, the only son of his mother; and she was a widow. And a large crowd from the city was with her. When the Lord saw her, He had compassion on her and said to her, "Do not weep." Then He came and touched the open coffin, and those who carried him stood still. And He said, "Young man, I say to you, arise." So he who was dead sat up and began to speak. And He presented him to his mother.

This is a wonderful psychological drama taking place in the human consciousness. The dead man in the Bible is the desire that you've failed to realize. You may have wanted to be a singer but said, "I can't do it; I don't know the right people." However, as you claim that you're now what you long to be and realize that the Almighty Power issues a song of triumph through you, then you're resurrecting the dead man within yourself.

Or you may have a lingering illness. As you affirm: "I am the Lord who heals you. I will come and restore your health and mend your wounds," you'll experience the miraculous healing power of God flowing through you. This Presence restores harmony, health, and peace to your entire being.

The eternal verities should be dominant in your conscious mind. When you enthrone godlike thoughts in your conscious-ness, they generate a lovely emotion, your heart becomes a chalice for God's love, and wonders begin to unfold in your life.

A long time ago, a friend of mine became paralyzed when a heavy machine fell on her. She had to learn to walk and talk again, but she realized that the Healing Power worked within her. She kept affirming her wholeness and complete health. She also got medical attention and blessed the doctors who helped her, because all healing is spiritual. She affirmed: "God gave me a voice, and I speak clearly and well. I counsel people and walk again." She repeatedly pictured herself walking and living a full life. She ultimately fully recovered and has been ministering to people for the last 30 years. She achieved that through the power of the Almighty.

We must never let our joy, peace, love, and faith in God die. That state of mind is the real death. We should instead starve our fear, ignorance, superstition, jealousy, envy, and hate. When fear dies, there's only room for faith; and when hate disappears, only love remains.

If we're fearful, we need to develop our faith. This journey always takes place first in the mind, for the body can't do anything or go anywhere unless the mind directs it. Consciousness or awareness is the only Power and Mover. Human consciousness is in perpetual motion, and the mind is always active—even when we're asleep.

The Bible says: "He [Jesus] commands and raises the stormy wind, which lifts up the waves of the sea . . . He calms the storm, so that its waves are still." *Jesus* is your awareness of the Divine Power within you that enables you to accomplish your objectives. He represents your knowledge and use of the laws of mind at all times everywhere. The *wind* represents the terror and anguish that seize you at times, causing you to vacillate and tremble with foreboding. The *waves* are the negative emotions of the mass mind, such as melancholy, hatred, and anger. When your mind is at peace, Divine Wisdom rises to the surface, and all turmoil is stilled. When you focus on God, the sea of peace flows through your consciousness, and you're serene.

What should you do when fear and limitation seize your mind? Realize that your savior is always knocking at the door of your mind. Perhaps you work for the government and say, "I can't make any more money because I've reached the maximum on the pay scale." You're experiencing the waves of confusion and doubt welling up in you. However, don't drown in these watery, negative emotions. Some arbitrary scale set forth by a government bureau can't limit you. Wake up the gift of the Divine within you!

The Presence that dwells within you has the solutions to all problems. It knows only the answers and doesn't recognize any insurmountable difficulties. Therefore, you're your own savior for the simple reason that the Supreme Intelligence is within you. Today's scientists know this truth: When they don't get an answer, they say, "Well, we didn't ask in the right way," for they know that the answer is already there before they seek it.

Realize first that the achievement of your desire is already a reality, even if you can't see the results yet. Then understand that by mentally uniting with your wish, you can calm the turbulent waves of fear and hesitancy. That's called *walking on the waters*. Your faith is your feeling and your awareness that the thing you're praying for is already a reality. Suppose you're working on an invention. Well, isn't it in your mind? Doesn't it have form, shape, and substance in the mental dimension? It can be seen by a good psychic even though you haven't yet committed it to paper because it's real in your mind. If you're writing a book, the chapters, characters, and story first appear in your mind.

Trust your mental picture, for it's real. As you focus your attention on your ideal, you walk on the waters and quiet the waves of fear. Then Infinite Power flows through that focal point of attention.

Keep your eyes on your goal and know in your heart that there's an Almighty Power that supports you in every way. It never deserts you. If you focus on fear, false beliefs, and error, you'll sink. Instead, look up and contemplate your desire, for you'll go where your vision is. With your eyes focused on God, there's no evil on your path. Your faith and confidence enable you to walk on the waters of life to green pastures. The winds and the waves will obey you because you possess spiritual knowledge and awareness.

The Bible describes a man who was possessed by a demon and was in great torment. Jesus commanded, "Come out of this man, you evil spirit!"

And Jesus asked the demon, "What's your name?"

"My name is Legion." the demon replied. "There are many of us."

Jesus allowed the evil spirits to flee from the man and enter 2,000 pigs roaming nearby. The pigs then ran into a lake and drowned. This story is symbolic, of course. The possessed man is someone who has permitted thoughts of remorse, hatred, revenge, self-pity, and anger to take charge of his reasoning, discriminating mind. These are the real devils that pursue us. We must never abdicate and let destructive emotions control us.

Because we can't visualize an emotion, we have to imagine our ideal in our mind, which generates the emotion. By redirecting our thoughts, we take charge of our emotional life.

I knew a man in New York who feared that whenever he went into a bar, some evil entity was lurking in the shadows, waiting to take possession of him. He'd been told or read somewhere that such demons are out there, and the poor man believed it. He didn't know that we create our own devils. This belief governed his mind and caused all kinds of trouble. He began to hear what he thought were the voices of spirits, not knowing that he was talking to himself. He thought that he was conversing with supernatural entities.

The man went to a priest, who conducted an exorcism to banish the tormentors. The ceremonial prayers of the priest instilled great faith and confidence in the subconscious mind of this man. He was extremely receptive to the power of the church and its leaders to cast out so-called devils. The priest also had confidence in his prayers, incantations, holy water, and so forth, and a marvelous healing took place. The priceless ingredient in the process was faith, which brought about a basic change in the mental attitude of the "possessed" man and generated a healing.

Many people dwell on the past—on an old lawsuit, the way someone treated them once upon a time, and things that may have happened 30 or 40 years ago. They don't know they're re-creating the same negative conditions for themselves through the law of mind: You manifest what you think about and imagine. When you talk about past failures, you attract more failure to yourself. Therefore, let go of events that are over and dead and anticipate the good that is to come, including health, happiness, and peace of mind.

When you refuse to acknowledge your prejudices, peeves, and grudges, these ideas are forced down beneath the conscious level of personality. When you nurse these negative thoughts, they sink into the unconscious area of the mind like an ember that sooner or later will explode. However, if you hold up your prejudices and jealousies to the light of reason and wisdom, they dissolve, and you're freed to lead a normal life.

It would be good for all of us to take a thorough look at ourselves and see if the qualities we criticize so harshly in others are not also in ourselves.

When you're asked to pray for people suffering from psychotic conditions, you can't get their cooperation because they don't have the capacity to reason and discriminate. When you do affirmative treatments for them, you need to do all the work yourself. You have to convince yourself of their freedom, peace, harmony, and understanding. Don't visualize them in a restraining bed or chair, but as healthy human beings. You can say the following prayer pray two or three times a day:

> *I now decree that the intelligence, wisdom, and peace of God manifests in these people and that they are free, radiant, and happy. The joy of the Lord is their strength. They are illumined from On High and are now in their right minds. The mind of God is the only real and eternal mind. This is their mind; and they are calm, relaxed, and at ease. They are full of faith in the Infinite Presence and Power and all good things. I decree this, I feel it, and I see them as whole and perfect now. Thank you, Father.*

This is a wonderful prayer to help people who are mentally imbalanced. By repeating these truths to yourself, realizing that there is but one mind, you'll facilitate a great healing. At no time should you give power to symptoms or the prognoses: You should instead have faith in the Infinite Presence, which always responds to your prayers. *I will restore health unto thee, and I will heal thee of thy wounds, saith the Lord.*

When you pray for someone, you leave the world of appearances and circumstances. You claim that the person's essence—the Divine Presence—can't be sick, confused, or insane. Nothing could ever harm the Living Spirit Almighty, which is boundless wisdom, absolute peace, and holy love. The individual you're treating for has all of these qualities. When you meditate on the Eternal One, the fixed opinions that separate people from God's river of peace and love dissipate.

The Bible says: "I will lift up mine eyes unto the hills, from whence cometh my help!" The hills refer to the God within you, the Source of all wisdom and power. The Bible also says: "Be still and know that I am God." Still the wheels of your mind and think of God and His love. Contemplate the river of peace and the joy of the Lord flowing through you. Your mind will settle and reflect the heavenly lights and truths. Constantly claim that God's wisdom, truth, and beauty guide you in all of your ways.

Whenever worry arises, realize that God hasn't given you a spirit of fear, but love, power, and a sound mind. God is guiding you now.

In a Nutshell

There's no one in the entire world like you, and God needs you where you are—otherwise, you wouldn't be here. Banish fear, doubt, and ill will from your mind. Trust the Divine Presence completely and say, "I have faith and confidence. I can do all things through the God Power that strengthens, comforts, and directs me." Then observe the wonders you'll perform.

When you begin to discipline your mind, don't permit the doubt, anxiety, or false impressions of the world to intimidate you. Instead, direct all of your thoughts constructively, for you have complete dominion.

Prayer is the contemplation of the truths of God from the highest standpoint. When you say, "God loves and cares for me" or "God is guiding me now," you're praying. And you'll always receive a response.

We must never let our joy, peace, love, and faith in God die. That state of mind is the real death. We should instead starve our fear, ignorance, superstition, jealousy, envy, hate, and other negative qualities. When fear dies, there's only room for faith; and when hate disappears, only love remains.

Realize first that your desire is already a reality even if you can't see the results yet. Then understand that by mentally uniting with your wish, you can overcome the turbulent waves of fear and hesitancy.

When you nurse thoughts of revenge and remorse, they sink into the unconscious area of the mind like an ember that sooner or later will explode. However, if you manage your thoughts intelligently, you can be free and lead a fulfilling life.

Whenever worry arises, realize that God didn't give you a fearful spirit but endowed you with love, power, and a sound mind. The Healing Presence in the midst of you is guiding you now.

Chapter Six

With God, All Things Are Possible

The stories in the Bible are psychological allegories and must be interpreted as such. For example, the New Testament describes how Jesus healed the little daughter of Jairus, a synagogue ruler who begged him to help. Jesus went to the bedside of the child (whom everyone believed to be dead), took her hand, and said, "Little girl, I say to you, arise." And she did stand up and walk, for she was completely healed.

In metaphysical terms, you're Jairus when you throw yourself at God's feet, knowing that only the Divine Healing Power has the solutions to your problems. *Jairus* also means "illumined reason," for those who know that God is omnipotent are enlightened.

The dying daughter represents your unfilled ambition—the desire of your heart. It may be perishing because you lack the faith to resurrect it, but when you go to Jesus or the Healing Presence, it can be restored.

When you begin to think about what you wish to express, the creative power of the Infinite responds. And by remaining faithful to your new mental focus, you'll resurrect your "child"—your idea or dream. You know in your heart that your aspiration isn't dead and that you can bring it forth.

In the same story, the Bible describes a woman who'd been suffering from a bleeding disorder for 12 years. No one had been able to heal her. When she saw Jesus in the crowd, she touched the hem of his garment, and immediately her bleeding stopped. Jesus said to her, "Daughter, your faith has healed you. Go in peace."

What does this allegory mean? One interpretation is that *woman* means emotion, feeling, or the subjective self. As we know, a woman who's bleeding can't conceive a baby. When our emotions run wild and are undisciplined—when we're full of fear, anger, hate, resentment, and self-condemnation—we're bleeding symbolically and can't manifest our desires. How can a person with such an attitude be healed? The Holy Spirit won't flow through a contaminated consciousness. The water in the pipe is waiting to come forth, but if the pipe is full of debris, rust, and corrosion, the flow of the water is blocked. Or if the water comes out, it's so polluted that we wouldn't drink it.

When you pray, you must forgive—yourself and everybody else. You must have a pure mind and an open heart, as the woman did when she touched Jesus's garment. Your mind is like a womb that must be protected for a baby to develop. As you go within and shut the door of your senses to all objective evidence, assume that you're already what you long to be. Realize that the power of God is backing you up and that nothing can oppose or challenge Him. Then you'll succeed in giving form to your idea or plan.

Faith is an awareness of the Presence and Power of God and His response. However, many people focus their attention on lies, superstitions, and erroneous concepts of all kinds. When we do this, confusion reigns supreme. Instead, we should turn to the Divine Presence within and realize that It is omnipotent and all-knowing. With our eyes focused on God, there's no evil on our path. When we have faith and mentally affirm the idea of perfect health, the Healing Power responds, and we're made whole.

☙✝❧

Isn't it true that your five senses mock you? Don't they challenge you and say that something can't be done . . . that it's impossible? Don't they tell you that the cancer has metastasized throughout your body and that it's incurable? This is why you need to suspend your senses and direct your mind to the new mental picture, realizing that with God, all things are possible. You need to go within, and the Infinite Intelligence will move on your behalf. In biblical language, you're touching the hem of the garment. *According to your faith, it is done unto you.*

As you envelop your desire with the mood of love, you become one with it and choose harmony, health, and peace. You wish for everyone happiness and all the blessings of life. You also realize that God is compassion and can't do anything unloving. His will for you is a greater measure of health, joy, and the gifts of heaven. *Bless the Lord, O my soul . . . Who heals all your diseases, Who Redeems your life from destruction, Who crowns you with lovingkindness and tender mercies, Who satisfies your mouth with good things, so that your youth is renewed like the eagle's.*

☙✝❧

When you say *I am,* you're announcing the Presence of the Living God within you—the Father and Mother of all creation. You realize that what's true of God is true of you. You have a sense of at-one-ment with your ideal and desire goodwill and joy for everyone. You adore and venerate the God within who created you from a cell. To love in that sense is to give all honor, recognition, and glory to the One Who Forever Is. It means having a healthy reverence for the Eternal Being that shapes your destiny. And when you love the Divine within yourself, you have respect for the Divinity within others.

In another parable in the Bible, a father begs Jesus to help his son, who seems to be possessed by an evil spirit. The boy was foaming at the mouth, gnashing his teeth, and having convulsions. The father beseeched Jesus, "If you can do anything, take pity on us and help us."

Jesus answered, "If you *can?* Everything is possible for him who believes."

Then Jesus rebuked the evil spirit, "You deaf and mute spirit, I command you, come out of him and never enter him again."

The spirit left the boy's body, and the son was completely healed.

Although the biblical passage doesn't mention the word *epilepsy,* given that the boy was foaming at the mouth and having convulsions, it's likely that he was suffering from this malady. The Greeks believed that epilepsy was caused by the moon, which in ancient symbology represented the subconscious mind. The Bible is therefore saying that the child had a subconscious poisonous pocket that provoked his seizures or epileptic fits.

Modern psychology and psychiatry have proved that mental and physical disorders have their roots in the depths of the subconscious mind, which they refer to as the *unconscious*. Negative subconscious patterns cause many kinds of illness. When the subconscious is sullied with hate, resentment, anger, and so forth, people go insane or have a nervous breakdown. They end up in the hospital because they're going against the stream of the Life Principle, which seeks to flow as harmony, beauty, love, peace, joy, rhythm, and order.

It doesn't really matter whether the child in this story was epileptic or not. What's important is realizing that with God, all things are possible.

The Bible says that illness can be healed through prayer and fasting. *Fasting* means abstaining from the evidence of the senses—from fear, ignorance, dogma, and superstition. We need a fast from the poisons of the world and the false beliefs of the mass mind. We also need to *feast* on faith in the goodness and wisdom of God, who is the same yesterday, today, and forever.

We prove our devotion and love for the Infinite by identifying ourselves with the Divine qualities and attributes and by absolutely refusing to recognize evil or illness as having any power over us. The Healing Presence is always seeking to express Itself through everyone as health, joy, beauty, and goodwill. Because of our faith in the One Power, we claim perfect harmony and peace.

A child grows in the image and the likeness of the mental and emotional climate of the home. For example, if a father and mother are fighting and abusing each other, the little baby in the cradle picks up on that and suffers from all manner of diseases. I've seen that happen a lot. However, when the parents pray together, honor each other's Divinity, and speak kindly, the child thrives in that atmosphere. He or she ceases to have skin irritations, asthma, fevers, and so many other problems.

The failure to bring about a healing is caused by an absence of faith in the mind of the person attempting to do an affirmative treatment. The illness or condition is actually gripping the practitioner, who hasn't awakened to the truth of the patient's perfection. When we're unable to achieve a healing, we've simply failed to fix our mind's eye on the person's embodiment of wholeness, beauty, and perfection. On the other hand, when we pray with faith, we get results.

⊰✦⊱

Many people have a deep, unconscious belief that certain maladies—such as psychosis, cancer, and things of that nature—are difficult to heal, When they see a mentally ill person with severe symptoms, they become fixated on the problem. However, we must completely detach ourselves from the evidence of the senses and identify with the Omnipotent Healing Presence within, paying no attention to appearances and symptoms. We have to heal the person in our own mind and come to the conclusion that God operates through that individual as harmony, peace, love, joy, intelligence, and wisdom. As we continue to do so, these healing thoughts are resurrected in the mind of the other person, who will experience a great recovery.

Here's a treatment or prayer that I use in treating disorders such as insanity, epilepsy, or whatever the case might be: I go within myself and mention the name of the patient. Then I think about the God Presence for three or four minutes, mentally dwelling on the Infinite peace and Divine love in the depths of myself. At the same time, I claim that whatever is true of the Infinite is true of the person I'm praying for. I try to achieve a feeling that the mind of the patient I'm treating for is harmonious. In this way, I induce the mood of peace, health, and serenity. When I feel that I've done the best I can, I stop and claim that the person is whole.

I repeat this treatment two or three times a day—or as often as I feel led to. I always pray as if I'd never done so before—with faith and enthusiasm. The main thing is to keep on keeping on until the day breaks and the shadows flee in my own mind. It requires persistence and refusing to take no as an answer. The main purpose of all prayers for others is to get the feeling of inward joy; God will do the rest. In prayer we must go to the sanctuary in our mind, which is that Infinite Intelligence in which we live and move. It's also a state of inner peace and rest. As we enter this place frequently, we shall see heaven on Earth.

⚑✝⚑

Know this . . . that there is a miraculous Healing Power within you. The uplifting, strengthening power of the Healing Presence is now restoring every atom of your being. The God within seeks to purify, vitalize, and make you whole. Have complete trust in the Infinite Healing Presence and know that It is bringing all of your affairs into Divine order. See and know that God is life and is manifesting through you now. This life is flowing through you harmoniously, peacefully, joyously, lovingly, and beautifully. Your every cell dances to the rhythm of the Eternal God.

Claim that the Infinite reveals itself through you as strength, purity, beauty, wholeness, perfection, and eternal youth. The rejuvenating power of the Almighty Spirit is now operating in you, making you pure, fresh, and radiant with Divine life. With every moment, you're growing stronger, healthier, happier, and more youthful. The vitalizing, tireless energy of God is flowing through you now, and you feel wonderful. The Mighty God, the Everlasting Father, and the Prince of Peace are within you. God created and sustains you, for He's the Living Spirit within—your consciousness and awareness.

Spirit has no face, form, or figure. It is shapeless and ageless. To worship is to give your supreme loyalty and devotion to the God within. You know in your heart the great truth that He is closer than your breath and nearer than your hands and feet. He is healing you now.

⚑✝⚑

The Healing Power was never born and will never die. Everybody in the world has the gift of healing, for the Infinite Presence is within all people. It's operating within you 24 hours a day, whether you're aware of It or not.

Have you ever considered all the cuts, bruises, and scratches you got when you were young? Did you notice the Infinite Intelligence at work? It closed up your cuts and created new skin and tissue. You've had hundreds of healings since you were born. These probably happened without your being aware of the process. In fact, the Intelligence within is constantly renewing your body. Faith causes this Divine Power to speed up tremendously— so much so that you can experience an instantaneous healing.

⊱✦⊰

Many people observe the Sabbath from a literal standpoint, thinking that it's a sin to drive a nail or do work of any kind on this "day of rest." The Sabbath can also be seen more figuratively as an inner stillness or silent knowing of the soul. It's the interval of time between your prayer and its manifestation.

You're in the Sabbath when you've accepted in your mind that your prayer has already been answered. You've reached the seventh day, which psychologically means the *moment of conviction*. Your heart is aflame with the glory of the Infinite and the certainty of Its response. At that moment, you'll experience an instantaneous Divine transfusion of energy, power, and life.

We must realize that the external acts, rituals, and ordinances of a church or other religious organization aren't true worship. You can observe all of the rules and regulations of your church and at the same time violate the laws of God in your heart. You can attend services every day of the week and still be very unreligious.

We must become aware of the fact that the only change that matters is the internal one: a transformation of the heart in which you've actually fallen in love with spiritual values. Religion is of the soul, not of the lips. Do you believe in the goodness of God in the land of the living? Do you glory in the joy of the Lord who is your strength. Do you know that the Infinite's will for you is life, love, truth, and beauty transcending your fondest dreams? If you have this kind of conviction, you have a wonderful religion.

The synagogue in the Bible represents your mind, where thoughts, feelings, moods, and opinions gather. When you're sick, you're suffering from a negative pattern of thoughts in your subliminal depths and are filled with fear and doubt. You must psychologically slay these thoughts by asking them where they came from. Are they not just shadows without heavenly credentials? Have you ever sat down and asked yourself about the source of the ideas you believe in? Are your thoughts true or are they illogical and unscientific? Do they insult the intelligence of a ten-year-old child?

Say to yourself, "I will not believe anything that does not conform to the eternal truths, for truth never changes; it's the same yesterday, today, and forever."

Dr. Fleet, a psychologist at the University of London, told me that during World War II, she was out on a street when a bomb hit a London hospital where some patients who'd been paralyzed for 18 to 20 years were staying. When the explosion occurred, they ran down the stairs and outside even though they'd been paralyzed. Some of the patients accepted the healing and can still walk today, Dr. Fleet noted. Others said, "I'm paralyzed; I shouldn't be walking." And, of course, they went right back to their paralytic state.

During the bombing emergency, the desire to save their lives seized their minds. They forgot that they were injured, and the Almighty Spirit began to move on their behalf. That Spirit is also within *you* . . . and you don't have to wait for a bomb to explode to discover it. Imagine that you're being healed now. Do this as often as necessary, and you'll rise and walk in the power of God.

⊱✛⊰

When the mind is full of stress, a corresponding effect is produced in the body, and the organs break down. If someone is possessed with hatred, fear, or deep-seated resentment, the mental poison he or she produces can corrode the body and cause organs to fail. For example, when Barry K.'s father died of kidney failure, Barry became extremely scared that the same thing would happen to himself. As I've noted before, that which you greatly fear will come upon you.

Barry began to experience symptoms similar to those that his father had felt in the early stages of his disease. He received some medication that helped quite a bit, but he was certain that he would have to start dialysis within a few years. After consulting with me, the truth began to dawn upon him that his fear was a perversion of the truth. Barry realized the truth about his situation and cast out the lie. He cooperated with his doctors but also reasoned that the Healing Power that created him was still within him. He knew that his disease was due to disordered thoughts; therefore, he began to change his ideas to conform to the Divine pattern. Before going to sleep at night, he would affirm the following with great feeling:

> *The Healing Presence is now going to work transforming, healing, restoring, and controlling all the processes of my body. There is no other power. I rest secure in this knowledge and know that Divine love and wisdom operate through me. I experience perfect health, harmony, and peace.*

He repeated this prayer with deep understanding and feeling every night for about 30 days. At the end of that time, his mind had reached a conviction of wholeness and health.

I attended a church service some years ago where the minister gave a very fine talk on Divine healing. After the service, a member of the congregation told him, "It's all right to say, 'Jesus heals,' but don't go claiming that we can do it." Can you imagine hearing a statement like that in this so-called enlightened age?! Look at the hospitals around the world. People with psychotic disorders are being healed, the disabled are learning to walk, and many suffering from epilepsy are being cured. People are also being healed at shrines, through the laying on of hands, and via other spiritual treatments. Your daily newspaper publishes many articles about cancer going into complete remission even after it has metastasized to the brain. We must remember that the Life Principle is forever mending our cuts, bruises, sprains, and scratches. Its tendency is to heal and restore.

A Christian Scientist told me that one time he swallowed a poisonous liquid by mistake. He was a splendid practitioner who had great faith in the God Power. He told me that he was 100 miles away from any kind of help, so he had to reply solely on the subjective power and wisdom within. He said that he got very still and prayed: "God is in His holy temple, and His Presence fills every organ and cell of my being. Where God is, there is only order, beauty, and perfect function. His Holy Presence neutralizes everything unlike itself."

He repeated this treatment for an hour, and although he became very weak, he eventually had a complete recovery. Could someone take a corrosive poison, trusting the Infinite Power to nullify its harmful effects? I don't recommend such an experiment, but I definitely believe that in emergencies such as this, the sincere student of truth can look to God with absolute faith and conviction and emerge from the experience unscathed.

⚜

If you believe that you're suffering because of sins you committed in a former life, you're making your own hell right here and now. It's a morbid belief. The past is over and remembered no more. You shouldn't question God and say it's His will for you to be sick or that He's testing you. That's absurd! So stop thinking that you have to atone for some wrongdoing from the past. Forgive yourself! Change your thoughts now, and the deeper mind will respond.

Believe in a God of love, and He shall wipe away all the tears from your eyes. There will be no more sorrow, pain, or confusion. God's will is beauty, love, harmony, joy, wholeness, and perfection. The Almighty One in the midst of you is guiding you now.

In a Nutshell

Your thought is creative. When you begin to think about what you wish to express, the Creative Power responds. By remaining faithful to your new mental focus, you'll manifest your idea or dream.

Turn to the Divine Presence within. Realize that It is omnipotent and all-wise. When you mentally affirm the idea of perfect health, understanding that the wholeness, beauty, and perfection of God are flowing through you now, the Eternal Power will respond and heal you.

We can observe all the rules and regulations of our church and at the same time violate the laws of God in our heart. We can attend services every day of the week and still be unreligious. We therefore must become aware of the fact that the only change that matters is the internal one: a transformation of the heart in which we fall in love with spiritual values.

Forgive yourself, for the past is over and remembered no more.

Change your thoughts now and the deeper mind will respond. You shouldn't question God and say that it's His will that you be sick. On the contrary, the Divine intention is harmony, beauty, love, peace, joy, wholeness and perfection. God in the midst of you is guiding you now.

Chapter Seven

The Doctor Treats; God Heals

*D*octors, psychologists, priests, and ministers don't heal anyone; they simply facilitate the Healing Power of God. For
example, surgeons can remove tumors, thereby releasing blocks
and clearing the way for the Healing Power to restore health. Psychologists and psychiatrists endeavor to remove mental obstruc-
tions and encourage patients to adopt a new attitude that will help
the Healing Presence flow through them as health, joy, and peace.
Ministers teach people to forgive themselves and others and to get
in tune with the Infinite, allowing love, harmony, and goodwill to
cleanse all of the negative patterns in their subconscious.

The nature of the Infinite is boundless love, unlimited intelligence, absolute harmony, and perfect peace. It has no beginning
or end. The Healing Power is present in every man and woman,
and It's dwelling in your heart now. Furthermore, healings take
place today just as they did thousands of years ago, for God is eternal and omnipresent.

⊰✛⊱

When you believe that God is testing or punishing you, you set
in motion the laws of your own mind, which will manifest trouble, sickness, and difficulties. You're actually punishing *yourself,*

for you attract experiences into your life—whether they're joyful or painful. Infinite Intelligence is the life within you, and when you understand the laws of your mind and apply them constructively, you're no longer blind.

I remember reading some years ago a statement Dr. Elmer Hess made when he was inaugurated as president of the American Medical Association. He said that a physician who doesn't believe in God has no business in a sickroom. I believe that most medical practitioners agree that faith in God has a profound effect on the maintenance of perfect health. The doctor treats the patients; God heals them.

You can perform what are called *miracles* in your own life. A miracle is a confirmation of that which is possible, for with God, all things are possible. Don't wait for some angel or saint to heal you. Don't wonder whether God wants you to be healed or not. *All things are ready if the mind be so.*

The first step in healing is to let go of your fear of what you're experiencing right now. The second step is to realize that your present conditions are simply the product of past thinking, which will have no further power to continue its existence. The third step is to exalt God, who wants to heal you. This process will halt the production of all the mental toxins that are hurting you. You lift your consciousness and see yourself as you want to be. Live in the embodiment of your desire, and what you wish for will soon manifest.

⛭✠⛭

Don't allow yourself to be swayed by the toxic thoughts that permeate the minds of so many people. Among the most deadly of these are fear, hatred (which is really ignorance), self-pity, and self-condemnation. These poisons seep through the psychic bloodstream, contaminating the wells of hope and faith and causing all forms of mental illness.

The spiritual antidote is to find the God within you and become intoxicated with the Divine Presence. You can fall madly in love with the new knowledge that thoughts are things and that by filling your mind with spiritual values, you can transform your entire life and experience health, happiness, love, and joy. You can become wildly enthusiastic, knowing that the law of attraction is forever operating in your life. Then you move forward in the light of the One Who Forever Is.

⛭✠⛭

The Bible says that as Jesus traveled to Jerusalem, he passed through Samaria and saw ten men suffering from leprosy standing far off. The men lifted up their voices, "Jesus, Master, have mercy on us."

Jesus told the men to go to the priests, and as they went, they were cleansed. When one of the men realized that he was healed, he praised God and fell to the ground offering thanks.

Jesus asked, "Were there not ten cleansed? Where are the other nine? Were there not any found that returned to give glory to God, save this stranger?"

Then Jesus said to the healed man, "Arise, go thy way. Your faith has made you whole."

This wonderful account of the lepers is a story about all of us. The word *leper* in the Bible means an unclean state. It indicates a mind troubled with conflicting desires and confused ideas. Leprosy is a wasting disease, as you know. Therefore, it typifies the state of people who've lost their vitality and enthusiasm for life because they've psychologically separated themselves from the Source of all life. We suffer from a leprous condition when we're full of envy, resentment, anger, hatred, and self-condemnation.

The cry of the ten lepers is the cry of the world. It's the appeal of every troubled, frustrated, neurotic person to the Master or Spiritual Power within, which alone can give peace of mind and health. As the lepers lifted up their voices, you lift yourself up mentally when you turn in reverence to the Spiritual Presence that heals all diseases.

The word *priest* is a symbol of spiritual perception, an intuitive awareness of the great truths of the Infinite. A priest is one who offers up a sacrifice, and each one of us is a priest of God when we turn away from the false gods of the irrational mass mind, with its fears and superstitions. We sacrifice our negative thoughts and false beliefs and contemplate love, peace, beauty, and perfection. We give up resentment, depression, and self-pity, and feast on joy, kindness, and harmony. We let go of ideas of karma and predestination and pledge our loyalty to the Eternal One, which doesn't condemn, punish, or send sickness and disease.

In the story, Jesus represents the ideal or desire that's always beckoning you onward and upward. Your vision is telling you, "Rise up and accept me." When you raise your desire in consciousness to the point of acceptance, you experience the truth of the statement: "Your faith has made you whole."

⊰✛⊱

All experiences in your life are the result of the interaction of your own subconscious and conscious mind. There's no other cause, power, or substance in the world. When these two are functioning harmoniously and constructively, it's a happy union. As you meditate on the spiritual values of life, you receive a transfusion of love, faith, confidence, and energy that courses through your veins and transforms your entire being. When your prayer is answered, you have peace and joy and are healed. All things are accomplished through faith in the creative laws of your own mind and the response of the Supreme Intelligence.

When you believe in good and evil, you're in a double-minded state and experience conflict and frustration. The battle is taking place in your own head. You don't know what to believe in because you're all mixed up. You look at your environment, circumstances, and conditions and tell yourself, "It's hopeless; I have a terminal illness." At that moment, you're saying, "God can't heal me." When you lament, "There's no way out; this problem can't be solved," you're claiming that God doesn't know the answer. In that instant, you're being an atheist.

Of course, these are absurd statements. You're transferring the power within yourself to external conditions. Perhaps you're blaming the weather, other people, or a jinx for your troubles. Maybe you're even blaming the stars. However, stars are just molecules moving in space. God created them and pronounced them good. There's nothing evil in anything—it just depends on what you do with it.

You must learn not to exalt a created thing above the Creator. You need to resolve the conflict by going within yourself and putting your case before the Great Tribunal: the One Presence and Power. In the secret chamber of your own mind, give supreme recognition to the Divine within. Look at the fearful, negative thoughts and order them out of your mind, realizing that they're only an *illusion* of power.

Remind yourself that there's only One Creative Power and that It is now flowing through your thought pattern, bringing you the good you seek. Keep on doing this regularly and systematically until a healing of the situation takes place. You've condemned the guilty (the negative thoughts) and freed the prisoner (your desire) into the arms of the Lord (your subjective self). Through repetition, faith, and expectancy, your desire has sunk deeply into your subconscious mind. The burden you've been carrying is now removed because you've discarded your old beliefs. You imbibe the light of God, knowing that only He knows the answer.

⇥✦⇤

We know that even if we've committed terrible crimes, we can instantly turn to the Presence of God within, claiming and feeling that we now are the person God intends us to be: a joyous, peaceful, loving individual. The law of God automatically responds to our new mental pattern, and the past is forgotten.

We're not talking about an idle prayer here. No! We're discussing a real transformation of the heart in which we desire to become a new person in God and long for Divine love and peace to come into our soul. Then the Spirit responds, for It's eternal and unlimited. As a result of Divine transformation, thieves and drug addicts are redeeming themselves and teaching others how to live according to the laws of God. *Blessed are those who hunger and thirst for righteousness, for they shall be filled.*

⇥✦⇤

The law of our mind never punishes us; we hurt *ourselves* through our misuse of the law. Ignorance is the only sin and is responsible for all the tragedy in the world. We merely experience a reaction of the law, which we set in motion with our thoughts and beliefs. When we understand this, we won't see a reason to resent or hate the meanest person who walks the Earth. In fact, there's no justification for harboring ill feelings toward people who cheat us, for nothing is lost unless we admit the loss in our mind. We only have to realize that all things exist in the Infinite mind. We must identify ourselves mentally and emotionally with what we want, and we'll be replenished from the Infinite reservoir of God's riches.

People who rob or otherwise deceive us are merely messengers telling us who we've conceived ourselves to be. They testify to our state of consciousness. How could we be angry or hostile to others when they're merely instruments of our own mind fulfilling the play that we wrote consciously or subconsciously in the book of life?

It's easy to forgive: All you have to do is absolve yourself for having negative, destructive thoughts that hurt you, while those with whom you were angry probably have been fishing, dancing, or having a glorious time. To heal any situation, claim that the Infinite Healing Presence is saturating every atom of your being and that Divine love flows through you, making you whole, relaxed, and perfect. Know and feel that the Living Intelligence that made you is in charge. You're now transformed because you've had a spiritual transfusion of the Healing Power released by your prayer, and your every cell dances to the rhythm of the Eternal God.

Negative attitudes are intruders in the house of God, for the Infinite One is peace, health, and joy. Emotions such as fear, worry, and anger are interlopers who rob us of our peace of mind. When we starve these states through neglect by giving all of our attention to the God Presence within, our mind is cleansed. At that moment we're exalting God, and we experience beauty, love, kindness, and inspiration.

It's true that many people are ungrateful. They'll tell you about the one disappointment they've had this year, but they won't describe the dozens of wonderful things that happened to them because of prayer or a change in their attitude.

Instead of complaining, we should give thanks and bless the name of the Lord. A grateful heart is always close to God because in giving thanks, we're uplifted and enter a state of receptivity. We're in tune with the Creative Power of the universe.

Harvey W. was in a Bible-study class I conducted. He said that he wanted to make significant changes in his life and begin to develop a quality that he was sadly lacking: thankfulness. Harvey said that he rarely praised anybody and that he wasn't grateful for his blessings. He was amazed when he began to consider all the wonderful things that had happened to him and the good fortune he enjoyed.

He quieted the wheels of his mind and began to imagine that he was talking to the King of kings within himself. In his mind's eye, he sensed the Divine Presence—his very essence—and began to say over and over again, "Thank you, Father, for my miraculous healing." He kept repeating this softly, gently, and lovingly. He would go to sleep every night in a mood of thankfulness, and he experienced a great healing.

We usually thank the salesperson when we order something. We know that the item will be sent to us, and we trust the organization implicitly. On a much grander scale, we should also give thanks when we do a spiritual treatment, knowing that the gift has already been given. The grateful heart rejoices in an answered prayer. We must learn to be a good receiver, for God lavishly

provides us with everything we want to enjoy. Go forth with gratitude because your desires have already been fulfilled.

We're all really pilgrims or strangers here. We've left paradise
and don't feel at home. Our pilgrimage is back to the Divine Presence. There's only one thing we're all seeking: the God within, the
One who lives in everyone's heart.

Consider something that's currently annoying you. Perhaps it's
a desire that hasn't been fulfilled. Turn to the God Presence within
and quiet your mind. Focus your attention on that fact that the
Spirit within you is God—the Cause and the Source of everything
good. Then silently say *Thank you* over and over again until you're
full of the feeling of gratitude. Let your prayer be: "God, give me
one more thing: a grateful heart." Continue to do this until your
consciousness is uplifted, and then your desires will be achieved.

There are many examples of miracles in modern times. For
example, there's the authenticated case of Madam Beret. She was
blind because her optic nerves had atrophied. She visited the
famous shrine at Lourdes and had what she termed a *miraculous
healing*. Journalist Ruth Cranston described what happened in an
article for *McCall's* magazine:

> At Lourdes she regained her sight even though the optic
> nerve was still lifeless and useless, as several doctors could testify
> after repeated examinations. A month later, upon reexamina-
> tion, it was found that the seeing mechanism had been restored

to normal; but at first, so far as the doctors could tell, she was seeing with non-functioning eyes.

Madam Beret wasn't healed by the famous waters of the shrine but by her expectancy and faith. She undoubtedly went to Lourdes knowing in her heart that she'd receive a healing. The Infinite Intelligence within herself responded to the nature of her belief, and her vision was restored. The Healing Presence that created her eyes could certainly bring the dead nerves back to life.

Some people have told me that they've experienced healings at the services I conduct on Sunday mornings. However, they say that they were skeptical and weren't even expecting a healing when they came to hear me speak. They seemed to lack faith, so how could they receive a healing? The answer is rather simple: They were seeking one, and their minds were open to receive the prayers of the multitude present at the service. Perhaps they were going to a doctor, osteopath, chiropractor, or psychiatrist for treatment, which is highly indicative that they desire to be healed—and desire is prayer.

When a group of people gathers in prayer—whether at a shrine or a church, or wherever—and affirm that all those attending are healed and made whole and perfect, they establish a definite psychological and spiritual link among all those present. Then, even if some of the people at the service are skeptics or unbelievers, it's still possible for them to be healed for the simple reason that they desire a healing. Their subconscious is receptive to the mental and spiritual atmosphere of the gathering, and a healing follows.

You might ask: What if someone is full of hatred, ill will, and resentment? Will that person experience a healing? Well, if a pipe is full of all sorts of debris, the water won't flow freely. Furthermore, the water that does get through will be muddy and contaminated.

It's necessary to remove the kink in the hose when watering a garden. Your body is the garden, and when you pray, you're infusing it with the Healing Power of God, releasing all kinks or blockages. The healing waters are love, peace, faith, joy, goodwill, confidence, and power. People who are full of hate block this stream of compassion and happiness. They must decide to let go of their grudges and pet peeves and let in the sunshine of God's love and healing. In short, a refusal to resolve mental conflicts definitely delays healing.

Millions of people are psychologically and spiritually blind because they don't know that they become what they think about all day long. They say that there's no way to solve their problems and that their situation is hopeless. They don't understand the workings of their subconscious mind and that whatever is impressed upon it—whether good or bad—will express itself on the screen of space.

We're also spiritually blind when we hate, resent, or are envious of others. We don't realize that we're actually secreting mental poisons that tend to destroy us. We begin to see clearly when we get a new perception of the mind, knowing that there is an Infinite Intelligence within us that's responsive to our thoughts and can solve all problems.

Men, women, and children across the land should be taught about the Creative Principle and how to use It. Everyone should be educated about the interrelationship of the subconscious and conscious mind and learn that life is responsive to their thoughts. Then they'll become anointed with the wisdom of God and do the work of the Divine.

⊨✛⊨

Age isn't the flight of years; it's the dawn of wisdom. Your gray hair should indicate wisdom and emotional maturity. In fact, the Spirit in you never grows old—It's the same yesterday, today, and forever.

⊨✛⊨

Ellen, who was suffering from incipient glaucoma, recently came to see me. I'd read an article some time ago about ophthalmologists in one of the larger hospitals who had discovered that in about 20 to 25 percent of the cases of glaucoma, the patients were carrying a burden of resentment or hatred. In fact, Ellen had a daughter-in-law whom she hated intensely. I advised her to pray for her daughter-in-law using these words: "I release my daughter-in-law unto God. I wish for her all of God's happiness, peace, and joy." She repeated this prayer frequently, until all the roots of irritation had withered in her mind. After a few weeks, she actually began to feel affection for the daughter-in-law. This is how true love melts everything unlike itself.

Ellen and I also prayed together frequently. She was open to the truth and used the following affirmation:

> *My eyes are God's eyes, and I see perfectly. The Living Intelligence that made my eyes is now controlling the processes and functions of my eyes and my entire body. I know and believe that my vision is spiritual, eternal, and indestructible. I see only the truth and God in all people and things.*
>
> *My eyes reflect the glory, beauty, and perfection of the Infinite. God looks out through my eyes, seeing His own ideas of perfection. My eyes are the windows of my soul. They are focused on love, truth, and beauty at all times. The vitalizing*

power of the Holy Spirit permeates every atom, cell, tissue, and muscle in my eyes, making them whole, pure, and perfect. The Divine perfect pattern is now made manifest in my eyes. Thank you, Father.

She let these truths sink into her deeper mind, and gradually a complete healing took place. She followed her doctor's instructions, and at the end of a few months, she no longer needed any medicine.

When you meditate or do affirmative prayer, you absorb these truths, and they become a living part of you. Just like the food you eat, your beliefs becomes tissue, muscle, bone, and blood. Realize that God is healing you now and that His peace fills your soul. *As a man thinketh in his heart, so is he.*

In a Nutshell

The Healing Power is present in all men and women. You can use It to perform what are called *miracles* in your own life. A miracle is a confirmation of what is possible. With God, *all* things are possible.

The first step in healing is to let go of fear of what you're experiencing right now. The second step is to realize that your present conditions are simply the product of past thinking, which will have no further power to continue its existence. The third step is to exalt God, who wants to heal you. As you lift your consciousness in this way, you'll manifest your desires.

All things are accomplished through faith in the creative laws of your own mind and the response of the Supreme Intelligence.

The moment you sincerely decide to change your life by enthroning a new concept of yourself in your mind, the law responds to the new blueprint you've created. This is the inner transformation that takes place.

As you focus on harmony, health, and peace, a rearrangement of your thought patterns takes place, followed automatically by molecular changes in your body structure that correspond to your new state of mind. You experience a spiritual transfusion, and every atom of your being dances to the rhythm of the Eternal God.

Focus on the fact that the Spirit within you is God—the Cause and the Source of all good. Then silently repeat *Thank you* over and over again until your mind overflows with the feeling of gratitude.

Chapter Eight

Living Without Strain

*D*r. Hans Selye researched the destructive effects of stress on the body's immune system. He observed that if the stress isn't temporary but persists week after week, the adrenal glands attempt to adapt to the situation by increasing their output of hormones and may ultimately become exhausted. This wreaks havoc on various processes in the body and lowers resistance. The individual may then develop arthritis, diabetes, or other diseases. Ultimately, he or she most likely will succumb to heart disease or cancer, which are today's greatest killers.

Dr. Selye's work also showed that the immune system can only effectively fight one thing at a time. If someone breaks a bone, the body quickly acts to repair it. However, if in the middle of this process, another stress such as fear is introduced, the healing is greatly impeded and disease may become chronic.

≒✛≓

You experience the same bodily symptoms when you face both real threats and imagined disasters. If you imagine yourself losing your job and being unable to pay your mortgage, you generate fears that set your endocrine system into action, releasing hormones that interfere with the chemistry of your body. You haven't actually developed an illness or had an accident, and there's nothing for these hormones to repair, so they cause problems. This is why Dr. Selye says that imaginary fears can strain the body and cause disease.

A young medical intern consistently worried about his future and was a nervous wreck. However, he learned to imagine himself filling a staff position in a big hospital and possessing a sumptuous office in the city. In his mind, he saw his friends congratulating him on his successful practice. He played this mental movie repeatedly. Whenever he began to feel worried or anxious, he purposefully flashed the pictures of his desires on the screen of his mind.

As the weeks passed, the Higher Power moved on his behalf, honoring his dreams and making them all real. The chief surgeon invited him to be his assistant, and in time, the young man earned a reputation for being a first-rate doctor and became wealthy. This is the way you can overcome the habit of worry and create what you want in your life.

You don't have to suffer from chronic anxiety. Don't spend time dwelling on your problems. Cease all negative thinking because your mind can't function harmoniously when it's tense. Instead, when you face a challenge, do something soothing and pleasant to relieve the strain: Take a drive, go for a walk, play solitaire, or read a favorite chapter of the Bible or an inspirational book to develop self-confidence and inner peace. Read it over carefully and quietly several times. You won't suffer from stress if you do these things. An inner calm will envelop you, and you'll feel peaceful.

Here's a wonderful thing for you to do every morning when you awaken: Turn to the God Presence within in prayer. Know that the Infinite Intelligence watches over you while you're sound asleep. Relax your body, then have a dialogue with the Higher Self. Become as a little child, which means that you trust the Divine Presence completely, knowing that It is healing you now.

The next step is to affirm lovingly:

> *Thank you, Father, for this wonderful day. It is God's day and is filled with joy, peace, happiness, and success. I look forward to it with a happy expectancy. The wisdom and inspiration of the Almighty will govern me during the entire day. The Infinite Intelligence is my senior partner, and everything I do will turn out wonderfully. I believe that Divine Wisdom is guiding me, and love fills my soul.*

The third step is to claim boldly:

> *I am full of confidence in the goodness of God in the land of the living. I know that Infinite Intelligence watches over me all day everywhere I go. I let go and am calm. I know that God is in action in all phases of my life, and Divine law and order reign supreme.*

Make a habit of doing this prayer process every morning before you go to work. When anxious thoughts come into your mind, substitute any of these spiritual thoughts, and you'll condition yourself to experience peace and tranquility.

Millions of people throughout the world are sick from worry and anxiety. They lack faith in the Infinite, always expect things to go wrong, and fret over many things that never come to pass.

They'll tell you all the reasons why something bad should happen, and not one reason why something good should occur. This constant tension debilitates their entire system, resulting in physical and mental disorders. To illustrate, a man once said to me, "I'm worried sick about my pharmacy. I may lose it. Business is good, but it can't last. I may go bankrupt, and I'm anxious about everything. My mind is in turmoil and I can't sleep because of my stress. I'm also upsetting my wife. How can I stop worrying?"

This man was actually managing his business well. He had a fine bank account and by ordinary standards, he was prospering. However, his constant negative imagery was robbing him of enthusiasm and energy. In addition, he was making himself weak and less able to meet any challenges that might come along.

I explained to this pharmacist that if he continued worrying, he'd attract the conditions upon which he was mentally dwelling. The only thing really wrong with him was the false belief in his mind. He'd forgotten that he personally could control his thoughts and his life. I gave him the following spiritual prescription to use regularly and systematically several times a day:

My business is God's business. God is my partner in all of my affairs. The Supreme Intelligence within me is prospering my business in a wonderful way. I claim that all those working with me in my pharmacy are spiritual links in its growth, welfare, and prosperity. I know this and believe and rejoice in their success and happiness. I solve all of my problems by trusting the Infinite Wisdom within my subconscious mind to reveal the answer to me. I rest in security and peace. I am surrounded by love. I know that all of my business relationships are harmonious. Infinite Intelligence shows me better ways in which I can serve humanity. I know that Infinite Intelligence indwells all my customers and clients. I work constructively with others; and we all enjoy happiness, prosperity, and peace. When any worry or fear comes into my mind, I immediately affirm: "I fear no evil, for Thou art with me."

He began to set aside about 15 minutes in the morning, afternoon, and evening for the purpose of reiterating these truths, knowing that by repeating them frequently, his thought patterns would be reprogrammed for success. When morbid thoughts came to his mind, he'd immediately affirm: "Divine love fills my soul." He told me that in one day he must have said "Divine love fills my soul" about a thousand times. Gradually, the neurotic thought pattern of chronic worry and anxiety that had dogged him completely dissipated, and he rejoiced in his freedom.

Some kinds of stress can actually be beneficial. Dr. Selye called this good stress *eustress*. For example, before an actor performs, he's naturally tense and accumulates a certain amount of energy. That's constructive. It's just like a clock: If you wind it too tightly, the spring breaks. But if you wind it the right amount, it ticks rhythmically and gives you the correct time.

You may be a little tense before you speak before an audience— I am, and there's nothing wrong with that. The minute you begin to talk, you become like the clock ticking harmoniously. You look at the audience and say, "I radiate love, peace, and goodwill to all of them; and the love of God enfolds them. Infinite Intelligence thinks, speaks, and acts through me. My words heal, bless, and inspire. They elevate and dignify the soul."

This affirmation does away with all stress, strain, and anxiety because you're filling your mind with Divine truths, and they crowd out everything unlike God. Furthermore, the audience is blessed.

To have peace of mind, you need to be creative, roll up your sleeves, and express yourself fully. You may get some blisters, but you're being constructive and are releasing your splendor. You're here to get involved, help other people, and release your hidden talents to the world. God gave you all of His attributes, qualities, and powers for you to use, whether you're a singer, dancer, doctor, or salesperson. Serving gives you inner peace and satisfaction. On the other hand, just endlessly resting and sitting in a rocking chair without doing anything causes frustration and neurosis . . . it's existing without living.

You're a spiritual being living in a material universe. You're not living in your body; the body is living in you as an idea. It's simply waves of light and isn't solid at all. Furthermore, your spirit and mind are the cause, while your world is an effect. Your physical self, environment, pocketbook, social status, and relationships with others are all a reflection of your habitual thinking and imagery. In other words, you're belief expressed.

I hear people say, "It's a rat race out there. The pressure is awful and I don't know if I can stand it. My nerves are jangled, I can't sleep at night, and I have to take tranquilizers." Others say, "I have to take four shots of whiskey in order to go to sleep at night" or "I come home so tense and exhausted that I have to drink a few beers." You've heard things like that.

If you want to overcome stress and strain, go frequently to the world of Spirit within you and claim beauty and inspiration. Affirm that the Almighty Power is moving through you; and you'll be refreshed, revitalized, and strengthened. *Call on me, and I will answer you. I'll be with you in trouble. I will set you on high because you have known my name.* The nature of Infinite Intelligence is to respond to you. Turn to It and claim these things, and you'll feel the dew of heaven moving over the arid areas of your mind, refreshing you. You'll receive the manna or spiritual food that invigorates and enlightens you.

If you're upset or worried, turn to the Eternal One within you. Focus on the absolute harmony, boundless love, and complete wisdom of the Divine Being Who causes the sun to shine and turns the Earth on its axis. Think of these great truths and realize that Divine law and order operates in your life.

In this way, you'll be able to grapple with all problems courageously. You'll say, "Every difficulty is outmatched by God. The problem is here, but Infinite Intelligence is here, too. Therefore, I am bound to overcome. I was born to win, and the Infinite cannot fail." Then you'll tackle your problem with faith and confidence instead of stress and strain.

Begin to meditate on the great immutable laws of life, and you'll be transported from tension and frustration to inner peace and serenity. *For great peace have they which love Thy law, and nothing shall offend them.* The law is: You become what you contemplate. Therefore, focus on the marvelous truths, and they'll become potent in your life.

Everything in the universe passes away. You can't be frustrated or sick forever, and you can't always be a square peg in a round hole. If it's hot, it's going to cool off; if it's raining, it's going to dry up. Remember that nothing is forever—that will give you a sense of tranquility. You can't be lonesome forever. Claim that Infinite Spirit is attracting to you a companion who will harmonize with you in every way, and it will come to pass.

There is a story about a Persian king who asked his advisors for a piece of wisdom that would always give him peace of mind.

What did they give him? A ring inscribed with the words "This, too, shall pass." Everything will pass away. If there's a war, eventually there will be peace.

Dwell on these lofty truths from the Bible: *If God is for me, who can be against me? All things are ready if the mind be so. According to my belief is it done unto me. Thou art ever with me, and all that I have is thine. Before you call, I will answer; while you are yet speaking, I will hear.*

Are you going to complain, "It's too hard for me"? The Bible says: "Do not be afraid nor dismayed . . . for the battle is not yours but God's." Every problem has a solution. Therefore, go within to the Infinite Intelligence, and the answer will come to you. If you're anxious about your income, family, or business problems, go to the Spirit that contains all love and wisdom. These truths lift you up above the petty things of life and set you free.

Where there's no judgment, there's no pain. You don't have to have opinions about the headlines in the morning or about John Jones shooting himself—you didn't tell him to do it. If you get agitated about it, you may suffer from stress and strain and develop ulcers or high blood pressure. You could instead say, "Well, he's with God, Who loves him and cares for him." You can do that even though he's committed suicide.

How can anything disturb you? You're disturbing yourself! It's not your job that's bothering you—that's not it at all—it's your reaction to your job that's the problem. If you resent the company or the boss and are reacting with hostility and anxiety, then of course stress enters your life.

Just do your work to the best of your ability, with love and goodwill. If you have lofty thoughts and dreams, you'll manifest them in all aspects of your business, relationships, and health.

✤

We're all here to put our hands to the plow and serve. You know in your heart that you're here to give. So, if you're living in an ivory tower, all wrapped up in reading metaphysical books and not expressing yourself, your life is out of balance. On the other hand, if you get overly involved in the external world and say, "Look, all I want is to make a lot of money and get ahead in life," you're also lopsided. You become a crass materialist and run to the psychiatrist for tranquilizers or hit the bottle—but they won't help you. When the drugs or alcohol wear off, you'll find that the disease is in your own mind.

You're here to lead a balanced life and live in both the subjective and objective worlds. You need to roll up your sleeves, whether you're digging in the soil or operating on a patient. Work with joy and love and go to the Father within regularly and systematically for refreshment, inspiration, and guidance. Then you're no longer imbalanced.

✤

If you're under too much stress, give yourself a break. Some people go off to the golf course for a few hours or take a trip for a day or two. When they come back, they're rested and have a quiet mind. Also say to yourself: "I can do all things through the God Power that strengthens me; I was born to win." Think of yourself as a child of the Infinite, and this will empower you. Realize that the Infinite can't fail and that tremendous Divine reserves are available.

No, you're not inadequate or weak. Develop a new sense of esteem for yourself and say: "I and my Father are one; the same Spirit that governs the planets and the stars is in me. One with the Infinite is a majority. If God is for me, who on earth can be against me?"

⇥✛⇤

The great American poet Walt Whitman wrote: "I am large, I contain multitudes," meaning that all the powers of God were within him. Most of us are unaware of the tremendous strengths we have. There have been many reports in the news about people discovering untapped reserves in times of emergency. For example, a woman weighing 90 pounds was able to lift the truck under which her husband had become pinned. Later, five men failed in their attempt to raise it. Where did her power come from? It was always there. Because she had an intense desire to save her husband's life, she was able to do it. She drew on the power of the Infinite and didn't even hurt herself.

In another case, a pedestrian saw a man trapped inside a car that was on fire. He ran over, pulled the door open, and carried the man from the blazing fire, walking away unharmed. Everybody was amazed. Where did that strength come from? It was always within him, and he called on it in an emergency.

Sometimes a surgeon thinks that an operation is going to be short but finds that it goes on for many hours. He has to draw on his reserves of energy, skills, and knowledge. The light of Infinite Intelligence guides and sustains him, and he pulls through.

You're also equipped to handle everything. You can never be presented with a problem that you can't overcome, because the Infinite Intelligence is within you. When you're named president or general manager of your company, the Life Principle in you knows that you can do the job—otherwise, you wouldn't have been promoted to the position. The Divine Power that moves the world is within you, and It only knows the answer.

A woman wrote a letter to me saying: "My husband sits around all day and does nothing but drink beer. He won't work, and he whines all the time. He worries me terribly, and my physician says that I have an anxiety disorder and am suffering from stress. On top of that, I have asthma, skin trouble, and high blood pressure. My husband is killing me."

In fact, her husband had nothing to do with her health concerns; it was her reactions to him that were causing her problems. I wrote to her and told her that today it's well known in the medical field that many skin disorders, asthma, allergies, heart conditions, and diabetes—as well as a host of other illnesses—are brought on by chronic worry.

I also gave her a spiritual prescription, suggesting that she bless her husband several times a day using the following affirmation:

My husband is God's man. He is Divinely active, prospered, peaceful, and joyous. He is expressing himself fully and is in his true place. He receives a marvelous income. Sobriety and peace of mind reign supreme in his life. I now picture him coming home every night, telling me how happy he is in his new job. I leave it all to the Infinite to fulfill.

I enclosed a second prayer, which she was to repeat with great emotion six or seven times a day until her subconscious absorbed it. I also advised her to picture her doctor telling her that she was whole and perfect. This is the second prayer:

The gifts of God are mine now. I use every moment of this day to glorify the Infinite. Infinite harmony, peace, and abundance are mine. Divine love flowing from me blesses all who come into my presence and is healing me now. I fear no evil, for the Infinite is within me. The sacred circle of God's love and power always surrounds me. I claim, feel, know, and believe definitely and positively that Divine love and eternal watchfulness guides, heals, and takes care of all members of my family. I forgive everyone; and I sincerely radiate love, peace, and goodwill to all people everywhere.

At the center of my being is the peace of the Infinite. In this stillness I feel the strength, guidance, and love of the Divine Presence. I am guided in all my ways. I am a clear channel for the light, love, truth, and beauty of the Eternal One. I feel the river of peace flowing through me now. I know that all of my problems are dissolved in the mind of God. His ways are my ways and are pleasant and serene. I rejoice and give thanks, realizing that my prayers are answered.

Sometime later she wrote, saying her prayers had worked wonders: "I've been saying the prayers as you suggested, and I've been holding a picture of my husband in my mind. He has found a job and is now sober. My doctor checked my blood pressure, and it was normal. All the blotches in my skin have cleared up, and I don't have to take asthma medicine anymore."

This woman's accumulated negative thoughts and mental pictures were the cause of her chronic illnesses. As she identified mentally and emotionally with the great truths given to her, they began to sink into her subconscious. She also painted pictures of health and vitality for herself and her husband. These mental images were etched in her deeper mind, which brought them all to fruition.

Once an executive came to me and told me that he was terribly worried that he wouldn't be named president of his company at the next scheduled board meeting even though he'd already been promised the position. His constant worry was about to give him a nervous breakdown. In talking with him, I concluded that he'd been anxious most of his life. However, he didn't agree with me and thought he was only worried about the possibility of not receiving a promotion. I advised him to picture himself as president and to imagine that his associates were congratulating him on his promotion.

He faithfully followed these instructions, and he was duly installed as president at the next board meeting. About a month later, however, he again came to see me because he was still feeling anxious. His doctor had told him that his blood pressure was dangerously high because of his stress. I noted that although he'd previously attributed his anxiety to his specific concern about not being named president, he still hadn't stopped worrying even though he'd achieved that goal. Now he was worrying that he might not live up to the expectations of the executive board, that his decisions might cause the company to lose money, and that he might be asked to resign.

He began to look inside himself. Suddenly he realized that all of his problems were caused by the fact that he didn't have a habit of praying and had no real contact with the Infinite Power from which he could draw strength and security. He'd thought that he was cursed with worries, but now he awakened to the truth that he alone was the creator of his stress and high blood pressure. As a result, he decided to establish a prayer practice to overcome his obsession. I advised him to use the following affirmation every morning:

> *I know that the answer to my problem lies in the Infinite Intelligence within me. I now quiet my mind. I get still and relaxed. I know that the Infinite speaks in peace and not in confusion. I am now in tune with It. I know and believe implicitly that God is revealing the perfect answer to me. I now live in the mood I would have if my problems were solved. I live in the abiding faith and trust that the solution is provided. This is the Spirit of the Infinite moving in me. It is Omnipotent. My whole being rejoices in the solution. I am glad, and I give thanks. I know that the Infinite has the answer, for with*

Infinite Intelligence, all things are possible. I know that God is the Living Spirit Almighty and is the Source of all wisdom and illumination. The indicator of the Divine Presence within me is a sense of peace and poise. I now let go of all sense of strain and struggle. I trust the Divine power completely. I know that all the wisdom and power I need to live a glorious, successful life are within me. I relax my entire body. My faith is in His wisdom. I claim and feel the river of peace flowing through me. I turn my request over to the Subjective Intelligence, knowing It has the answer. I am at peace.

He repeated the above prayer three times each morning, knowing that through repetition, these truths would sink into his subconscious and create a healing. He also realized that he now was anchored to the Divine Power within him. His sense of union with the Infinite gave him confidence to overcome anything that he'd mistakenly worried about. Through this shift in his mental attitude, he became a balanced man and let go of worry.

A woman once visited me and said she was always worrying about her son. She feared that he might get the measles, fall into a swimming pool, or be run over by a truck. She told me, "I can't stop worrying, and it's causing me a lot of stress."

I told her that it would be much better to bless her boy rather than to throw mental bricks at him all day long. I suggested that she open her mind, let in the Higher Power, and realize that the Infinite Presence and Power loves her son and watches over and protects him.

As she practiced blessing her boy, she cast out all her gloom and misery. She developed a habit of praying and no longer allowed destructive thoughts and images to influence her mind.

You can heal yourself as this woman did, by lifting up your

thoughts to God. Do this regularly and you'll be released from vexation and worry.

When you worry, you're using your mind negatively and destructively. You're creating conditions, experiences, and events that disturb you. However, you can overcome this pattern of thinking. Remember that fear is a shadow in your mind. When you welcome the light of Supreme Intelligence into your consciousness, the shadows flee. When you're perplexed and confused about what decision to make, don't get tense about it. Remember that you have an Inner Guide that will direct you and reveal the perfect plan to you.

The secret is to mentally devote yourself to the right answer until you receive it. The Infinite Intelligence deep in your subconscious mind is responsive to your request. You'll recognize the response as an inner feeling or overpowering hunch that will lead you to the right place at the right time, put the perfect words into your mouth, and cause you to do exactly what's needed. This releases you from strain and stress.

David L., a businessman, described to me how he prays for guidance. He has a rather simple technique: He goes into his private office where he won't be disturbed, closes his eyes, and thinks of the attributes and qualities of the Infinite, which he knows are all within him. This does away with all worry and tension and generates a mood of peace, power, and confidence. He moves from the material world to the spiritual one, where all is harmony and bliss. Then he speaks to his Higher Self: "Father, Thou knowest all things. Send me the idea I need."

He then imagines that the answer he desires is flowing through his mind and affirms: "I accept the response. Creative ideas unfold within me, bringing me harmony, health, and joy."

After this prayer, he gets busy with routine matters, and the answer inevitably reveals itself when he isn't thinking about it. David says that often an idea comes like a flash and startles him.

The answers are also within *you*. Divine Spirit reveals the solutions to you, allowing you to overcome frustration and anxiety.

The Bible says: "Choose for yourselves this day whom you will serve." The key to health, happiness, peace, and abundance lies in the capacity to choose. When you learn to think correctly, you'll stop choosing pain, misery, lack, high blood pressure, and limitation. On the contrary, you'll select from the treasure-house of the Infinite within you. You'll affirm decisively: "I choose happiness, peace, prosperity, wisdom, and security today and every day of my life."

The moment you come to this definite conclusion in your conscious mind, your subconscious, full of the Power and Wisdom of the Infinite, will come to your aid. You'll be directed, and the path of achievement will be revealed to you. Claim without the slightest hesitation or fear: "There is only One Power of Creation. It is the Power of my deeper self. There is a solution to every problem. This I know, decree, and believe."

As you boldly claim these truths, you'll receive guidance pertinent to all of your undertakings, and wonders will unfold in your life.

An engineer named Phil said to me, "I've been working for the same boss for over 15 years and haven't been promoted. My talents are being wasted, and I'm frustrated and unhappy. I hate my boss, and I have high blood pressure and ulcers."

Phil felt that he'd never advance in his work because of his age and his lack of good interpersonal skills. Together we delved into his past. He was brought up by a tyrannical, puritanical father with typical New England traditions. He'd resented his dad and hadn't been in touch with him for many years. Moreover, he felt guilty about hating his dad so much. He said to me, "I suppose God has it in for me."

Slowly but surely he began to see that he was rebelling against his boss in the same way that he'd rebelled against his father. It began to dawn on him that he was actually blaming his own shortcomings, mistakes, and misdeeds on his supervisor. In other words, the boss was a father image.

Phil overcame his sense of frustration by first perceiving that he was actually blocking his own promotion with his fears and resentment. He also realized that his ulcers and high blood pressure were due to his antagonism and stress. He decided to begin praying in the morning and evening as follows:

I wish for everyone at my job health, happiness, peace, and promotion. My employer congratulates me on my work. I paint this picture in my mind regularly, and I know it will come to pass. I am loving, kind, and cooperative. I practice the golden rule, and I sincerely treat everyone in the same way that I would like to be treated. Divine Intelligence rules and guides me all day long, and I am prospered in all my ways.

As he saturated his mind regularly and systematically with these thoughts, he succeeded in bringing about a new mental attitude, which made everything in his life better. Gradually his ulcer disappeared, and he no longer had to live on milk, toast, and things of that nature. His blood pressure dropped once he accepted that it had been elevated only because he felt that he was inadequate and resented those around him.

⊱✝⊰

Say to yourself: "I am always poised, serene, and calm. The peace of the Infinite floods my mind and my entire being." Practice the golden rule and sincerely wish peace and goodwill for all people. You won't suffer from stress if you do that. Know that the love of all things good penetrates your mind and casts out all fear and strain. You're now living in the joyous expectancy of the best, for only the best should come to you. Your mind is free from all worry and doubt. Your words of truth dissolve every negative thought and emotion within you. You open the doorway of your heart to the influx of the Holy Spirit. Your entire being is flooded with the light and understanding from within, and petty matters no longer irritate you. With your eyes focused on God, there's no evil on your path.

In a Nutshell

People experience the same bodily symptoms whether or not their fears are "legitimate." The adrenal glands secrete hormones when people become anxious about real threats and imagined disasters.

You don't have to suffer from chronic worry. Don't spend time dwelling on your troubles and cease all negative thinking, for your mind can't function harmoniously when it's tense. It relieves stress to do something soothing and pleasant when you face a problem.

You're here to express yourself, get involved, and release your hidden talents to the world. God gave you all of His attributes, qualities, and powers, and you're here to use them and give life to your desires.

If you want to overcome stress and strain, go frequently to the Spirit within you and claim that the Almighty Power is moving through you. You'll be refreshed, revitalized, and strengthened.

When you're perplexed and confused about what decision to make, don't get tense about it. Remember that you have an Inner Guide that will lead and direct you in all your ways, revealing to you the perfect plan and showing you the way you should go.

The Bible says: "Choose ye this day whom ye shall serve." The key to health, happiness, peace, and abundance lies in the capacity to choose. When you learn to think correctly, you'll stop choosing pain, misery, lack, high blood pressure, and limitation. On the contrary, you'll select from the treasure-house of the Infinite within you. You'll affirm decisively: "I choose happiness, peace, prosperity, wisdom, and security today and every day of my life."

Chapter Nine

———— •◦• ————

The Fallacy of Old Age

The United States is a wonderful country in which to be young. In fact, we idolize youth. But now it's going to be a great place to grow old because a large percentage of the population is reaching the age of 65 and older. These seniors are active in politics and are making their needs known to the people. This is fortunate because we need their experience and wisdom in government, science, business, and the arts. They offer knowledge and understanding garnered through years of living. As the Bible says: "In all your getting, get understanding."

However, many people haven't yet come to the realization that old age can be valuable. For example, some years ago I called on an old friend in London who was very ill. He said to me, "We're born, we grow up, and we become old and useless. That's the end." His attitude of futility and worthlessness was the chief reason for his sickness. He was frustrated, weak, and almost lifeless. He felt that because of his advancing years (he was over 82), he had no hope. He believed that no one cared about him, and he was looking forward to death.

Unfortunately, many people have the same attitude as my friend. They're afraid of old age and death. This really means that they're afraid of life, for we're eternal. Life has no beginning or end. The Spirit was never born and can never die. Your body is the garment that God wears when He takes human form. Your physical self is the instrument through which Spirit functions on this plane. When you finish this incarnation, you put on a fourth-dimensional body, for there's no end to the glory that is the human being.

Life is a progression. The journey is ever onward, upward, and godward. All things in the universe gradually return to the formless. And the formless is forever taking new shapes.

People who believe that the earthly cycle of birth, adolescence, maturity, and old age is all there is to life are indeed to be pitied. They don't feel that life has meaning, and this belief causes a sense of hopelessness that results in neurosis and all kinds of disease. As we age, we need to instead develop our awareness of the Presence and Power of God and a deeper faith in the response of the Supreme Intelligence to our conscious thinking.

Old age isn't tragic. It's simply change and should be joyfully welcomed, for each phase of human life is a step forward on the path that knows no end. We have powers that transcend our bodies and abilities that go beyond our five senses. Scientists in academic laboratories throughout the world are setting forth indisputable evidence that we can leave our physical self; travel thousand of miles; and see, hear, touch, and speak to people even though our body is on a couch far away. Totalitarian countries are using this astral projection for purposes of espionage and other forms of detection—this fact is well known by our defense department.

People are going to great lengths to appear young, including getting cosmetic surgery. However, they're denying the sovereignty of the One Presence. You'll always remain young if you think from a spiritual standpoint, for the Spirit never grows old. Just focus on whatever is true, lovely, just, pure, honest, and good, for the joy of the Lord is your strength.

The greatest antiaging technique is seeking the peace in the Divine center within yourself. Tune in and feel it now. All of the barbs, criticism, and hatred aimed at you will be absorbed, neutralized, and dissolved in the great ocean of God's love and harmony. This is the secret of remaining young forever. For instance, President Herbert Hoover was very active into his 80s, working on special assignments for the government. He was healthy, happy, vigorous, and full of life. His mind was clear and decisive. In fact, his mental acumen was sharper than when he was 40. He was a religious man—a Quaker—and had great faith in God, life, and the universe. He was subjected to a barrage of criticism during the Depression years, but he weathered the storm and didn't grow old with bitterness and resentment.

Some people are old, bitter, and sarcastic at 30, while others are young at 80. They're full of joy and laughter and spend their time painting, swimming, dancing, writing, sculpting, teaching, and doing all kinds of marvelous things. It's wonderful to behold. The great law of life is: *As a man thinketh in his heart, so is he.*

Enthusiastic people continue to be productive as they get older. For example, Dr. Valerie L. was still an active surgeon at 83. She operated every morning, visited patients in the afternoon, and taught courses at a medical college. She was full of joy and goodwill. Valerie loved her work and said to me, "If I should die tomorrow, I would be operating on people in the next dimension of life."

Other people have also achieved great things later in life. For instance, Giuseppe Verdi wrote his opera *Otello* when he was 74. The Methodist leader John Wesley was extremely active in expounding his convictions about God and His laws well into his 80s—he was burning with the zeal and enthusiasm of the Spirit. And Irish dramatist George Bernard Shaw continued to write until his death at the age of 94.

Some people try to recapture their youth by flitting from bar to bar or by trying to keep up with their kids in a ball game or swimming. However, this doesn't work because we can't keep up the pace we had as a teenager or beat our children to the top of a mountain. During the latter stages of life, nature forces the body to slow down. This is the God Presence saying: "We want you now to engage in mental and spiritual communion with the Divine. Then you'll accumulate years without aging. You'll experience joys that youth can never know because you're communing with the God Spirit that was never born and will never die." Therefore, don't be overly concerned with your body and appearance, for you're here to express all of the qualities and attributes of God and develop spiritual maturity.

As you enter into meditation with the Eternal One, say: "God's love fills my soul, God's peace floods my mind, God's light illumines my path, and God's power flows through me." Then you won't be trying to recapture your youth but will be connecting with the Presence that animates, sustains, and strengthens you.

If your body has slowed down and you can't play a game of tennis or swim as fast as your son or daughter, remember that Spirit is always clothing Itself anew. What we call *death* is but a journey to a new city in another mansion of our Father's house.

Our voyage is ever onward, upward, and godward. We go from glory to glory, strength to strength, and wisdom to wisdom, for we're part of the Infinite Spirit.

Time is relative. When Einstein was asked what time was, he said, "It's like this: If you're talking with a beautiful girl, an hour seems like a minute. But if you sit on a hot stove for 30 seconds, it feels like an hour." Time is our thoughts, feelings, and state of consciousness.

I met a woman in Beverly Hills who'd been in a Nazi concentration camp during World War II. Her relatives had all been killed by the Germans, but I've never met a more gracious, spiritual, sweet woman. She was 75 years old but looked about 40. She'd gone through the tortures of hell and had been beaten, kicked, and spat upon, but she'd reacted with love. She prayed for her captors and believed that God would lead her out in Divine law and order. She didn't grow bitter and hateful, for these are the qualities that cause people to become decrepit.

How could you ever say "I'm old and useless"? Never in eternity could you exhaust the glory and beauty in you, for you contain the God Presence. Remembering this will keep you young, vibrant, and full of the Light that never dims. You can't be less tomorrow than you are today, for life doesn't go backward, nor does it tarry with yesterday. Realize that the Divine in you is sovereign, and don't neglect your spiritual life.

⊰✦⊱

The Life Principle is forever seeking expression through you. It's the Eternal, All-Wise One. Give all of your power to the Spirit within that doesn't die. Nothing can oppose or vitiate It. Don't ascribe power to things, people, and events, for that makes you weak and anemic. Don't say "She's blocking my good" or "He prevents me from getting a job." In actuality, other people have no power over you; only God Almighty does.

⊰✦⊱

Many people become crotchety, irritable, gossipy, and inflexible. These are signs of old age. If you're 20 and are cantankerous and edgy, you're already very old. But if you're kind and gracious and enjoy the laughter of God, then you're young no matter what your chronological age is. When you're full of faith and have confidence in the only Power there is, you remain exuberant.

⊰✦⊱

Diets, exercises, yoga postures, breathing through your nostrils, and techniques of all kinds won't keep you young because they're external measures. When you start with your body, trying to recondition it through athletics and things of that nature, you're just kidding yourself. In fact, the Spirit is conditioned by *thought*. If your thoughts are focused on what is beautiful, noble, and good, you'll be young regardless of your chronological age. As you think godlike thoughts, your breathing will change. Every cell of your body will develop a radiant beauty that eating grapes, carrots, and other health foods won't bring you. You must therefore eat the bread of life: peace, joy, love, and inspiration.

We grow old when we lose interest in life and cease to dream about new truths and worlds to conquer. However, when our mind is open to fresh ideas and interests and we raise the curtain and let in the sunshine, we'll always be young and vital. For example, I was introduced to a man in Bombay many years ago who said that he was 110 years old. He had the most beautiful face I've ever seen and seemed transfigured by the radiance of an inner light. There was a rare beauty in his eyes indicating that he'd grown old with gladness.

※✟※

If you're 99, realize that you still have much to give. You can help guide the younger generation and offer your knowledge, experience, and wisdom. You'll find that you can never cease to unveil the glories and the wonders of the One Who Forever Is.

※✟※

The newspapers are taking cognizance of the fact that the senior population in California and other states is increasing by leaps and bounds. This means that their voice will be heard in the state legislatures and in the halls of Congress. Federal laws have been enacted prohibiting employers from discriminating against men and women because of age. Now there's a law that discourages businesses from laying off older workers when they cut staff members.

No one should be asked to resign when they reach 65 because that's the time of life when they could be most useful in handling personnel problems, making plans for the future, and coming up with creative ideas based on their experience and insight into the nature of the business. I know that some of the engineers who come to my lectures on Sundays are 75 or 80 years old. They're contributing their engineering abilities and understanding to society. There's nothing wrong with their ideas—they're marvelous.

I meet men and women who tell me that some employers slam the door in their face when they say that they're over 40. One man told me that a company wouldn't hire him because he was 36 and they didn't want to pay a few dollars more for insurance premiums. The total emphasis seems to be on youth, which is absurd and shallow and has to change. If the employer would stop and think, he or she would realize that the applicants aren't selling their age; rather, they're offering their talents, experience, and wisdom gathered through years spent in the marketplace of life. Thus, a person's age should be a distinct asset to a corporation, for someone with emotional and spiritual maturity is a tremendous blessing to any organization.

It's stupid beyond words to tell people that they can't be hired because they're older. It's like saying that they're ready for the scrap heap. What are such individuals to do? Bury their talents? Hide their light under a bushel? Those who are prevented from working because of age must be sustained by the government treasury at county, state, and federal levels. The very organizations that refuse to hire them and benefit from their wisdom and experience are taxed to support them. These companies are biting off their nose to spite their face. It's a form of financial suicide.

We're here to be producers, not prisoners of a society that compels us to be idle and puts us on welfare. Our body slows down gradually as we advance in years, but the mind doesn't have to grow old. In fact, it can be much more active at the age of 90 than it was at 9 or 20. It can be alert and quickened by the Holy Spirit.

There was a time in your life when you were happy and everything was provided for you. You played in the sand and were surrounded by your loved ones. These dear people are still all around you—you're only separated by energetic frequency. If you were psychic or clairvoyant, you'd see them. In fact, you may occasionally glimpse them in your dreams.

Psychics tell me that they sometimes see spirits on my podium when I'm speaking, and they describe them in detail. These spirits are people I've known, but whom I'm sure the psychics have never met before. Do you think that's strange? Well, there's nothing odd about it—not a thing.

Life is about expansion and development, and your loved ones are growing and expanding in the next dimension of life; they can never go backward. For example, if you're in the eighth grade, you can't return to the first grade, for that would be contrary to the laws of nature. Life goes from glory to glory, ever upward.

In God, there's fullness of joy and no darkness at all. Feel the miraculous Healing Presence moving through your mind and body. Know that you're inspired, lifted up, rejuvenated, and strengthened. Then you'll feel a deep response and become spiritually recharged. You can bubble over with enthusiasm and joy as in the days of your youth for the simple reason that you can always recapture that joyous state mentally and emotionally. Divine Intelligence reveals everything you need to know and enables you to affirm the presence of your good regardless of appearances. You walk in His light and all shadows flee.

Instead of saying "I'm old," proclaim, " I am young and am wise in the ways of God." You're not a failure, for you know that God never stumbles. You were born to succeed, so don't let the mass mind tell you that you're becoming old, senile, and useless. Reject those beliefs, for they're a lie. Affirm life, not death. Realize that you live forever and that Spirit is your reality. Envision yourself as happy, radiant, successful, and full of the light of God.

If you're retired, don't say, "I'm finished . . . I'm tired and old." No! You'll need to put new tires under the old chassis and perhaps do somewhat different work, but stay active and present. Become interested in the Bible, the Koran, the Talmud, or other religious or philosophical works. Delve into them for their inner meaning. Get a new vocation or do something you've always dreamed of. Go to the university and take up subjects you've always wanted to study. Travel, explore, investigate . . . and pray as follows: "As the deer pants for the water brooks, so pants my soul for You, O God."

Make sure that your mind never retires, for it's like a parachute that's no good unless it opens. Be receptive to new ideas, for God dwells within you As the Bible says: "His flesh shall be young like a child's; he shall return to days of his youth. He shall pray to God and He will delight in him."

In a Nutshell

Many people are afraid of old age and death. This really means that they're afraid of life, for life has no beginning or end.

Old age isn't a tragic occurrence. It's a change that we should joyfully welcome since each phase of human life is a step forward on the path that knows no end.

What we call *death* is but a journey to a new city in another mansion of our Father's house. Our voyage is ever onward, upward, and godward. We're part of the Infinite Presence that was never born and will never die.

When you focus on that which is true, lovely, just, and pure, you'll always remain young, for these qualities never grow old. The joy of the Lord is your strength.

As you think godlike thoughts, your breathing will change and every cell of your body will take on a radiant beauty that eating grapes, carrots, and other health foods won't bring you. You must therefore partake of the bread of life, love, and inspiration.

If you focus on Spirit, you'll maintain the sweetness of your ways as you move from youth to age.

Chapter Ten

You Need Never Grow Old

*M*ost normal people dread seeing the signs of old age appear in their body and want to remain as vibrant and robust as long as possible. Yet the majority of the population doesn't take sensible precautions to preserve their youth and vigor. They violate the laws of health and longevity and sap their vitality through foolish, unnatural habits—and then wonder why their energy is decreasing. Their physical selves pay the penalty for their abuse.

It seems strange that although we all love life so dearly and cling to it with such desperate tenacity, we deliberately throw away so many precious years through wrong living and bad mental programming. The human being is like a fine clock: If properly cared for, it will keep splendid time and run for a century, but if it's neglected or abused, it will wear out long before it should. If we made as great an effort to retain our youthfulness as many of us do to amass a fortune, we could stay energetic and enthusiastic throughout our lives.

※✦※

Perfect health is impossible for those who labor under the belief that they're on a physical decline and that their strength is gradually diminishing as they get older. As long as you dwell on thoughts of aging and images of infirmity, you'll grow old quickly. Your convictions will work against your real desire to stay youthful, just as thoughts of poverty counteract your wish to become prosperous.

On the other hand, if you focus on eternal youth and declare that the truth of your being—the Divinity within—can't age, you won't get old prematurely. The habitual thought of vibrancy will manifest itself in your body as harmony, beauty, and grace instead of wrinkles and feebleness. You're as young as your spirit, and your face can't betray the years until your mind has given consent.

⇥✦⇤

Most of us don't realize that our mental attitude is constantly creating results, and we don't understand how impossible it is for us to go beyond our self-imposed limits and do what we believe we can't. The idea that our energy must begin to decline and that the fires of ambition will die out after we reach a certain age has a most pernicious influence upon the mind. We actually *think* ourselves into old age—our convictions force us into it—and we'll go in that direction until we change our thoughts and transform our attitude.

We're not old until our interest in life has evaporated, our heart becomes unresponsive, and our enthusiasm wanes. As long as we're involved in the many aspects of living and are in touch with the developments of our times, we can't grow old.

⇥✦⇤

Some years ago, a well-known attorney committed suicide on his 70th birthday. A popular book about life and death was found beside his body. It included a passage from Psalm 90: "The days of our years are threescore years and ten; and if by reason of strength they be fourscore years, yet is their strength labor and sorrow; for it is soon cut off and we fly away."

In his suicide note, the attorney wrote: "I'm seventy—three-score and ten—and I'm now fit only to sit by the hearth and wait to die."

This man had dwelled for so long on the idea that we're useless and a burden to ourselves and the world after the age of 69 that he'd made up his mind to end it all when he turned 70. Yet it's unlikely that the psalmist had any intention of setting a limit on the acceptable life span or that he had any authority for doing so. Many of the sayings in the Bible that people take so literally and accept blindly are merely figures of speech. As far as the Bible is concerned, there's just as much reason for living to be 120 or even for reaching for Methuselah's age (969) as there is for surviving only until the age of 70. In fact, the spirit of the Bible encourages longevity through sane and healthful living. It emphasizes the duty of leading a useful and noble life and making as much of ourselves as possible—all of which tends to prolong our years on Earth.

We don't always realize what slaves we are to our mental attitudes and what power our convictions have to influence our lives. Multitudes of people undoubtedly shorten their lives by many years because of their deep-seated convictions that they won't live beyond a certain age—perhaps the age at which their parents died. How often we hear someone say, "I don't expect to live to be very old because my father and mother died young."

We're strongly affected by our self-imposed convictions, and it's well known that many people die very near the limit they set for themselves. For example, not long ago a man in New York told his relatives that he was going to die on his next birthday even though he was in perfect health. On the morning of his birthday, his family became alarmed because he refused to go to work, saying that he'd certainly die before midnight. They insisted on calling in the family physician, who examined him and said that there was nothing the matter with him. But the man refused to eat, grew weaker throughout the day, and actually did pass away before midnight. The conviction that his life was going to end had become so entrenched in his subconscious that the entire power of his mind acted to cut off his life force.

Now, if this man's conviction could have been changed by someone who had sufficient power over him, or if he'd implanted in his mind the idea that he was going to live until a ripe old age, he probably would have lived many years longer.

❆✠❆

If you've been taught or have convinced yourself that you'll begin to show signs of age in your 50s, lose your mental acumen and your interest in life in your 60s, and will then have to retire from your business and continue to decline until you're incapacitated, there's no power in the world that can keep you from becoming old and infirm. After all, the expression of age in the body is the harvest of ideas that have been planted in the mind. You see others about your age beginning to suffer, and you imagine that it's about time for you to develop the same problems.

To think constantly of "the end" and to plan for death and declining years is simply to acknowledge that your powers are waning. Such thinking tends to weaken your hold upon the Life Principle, and your mind gradually fulfills your conviction.

If you instead refuse to grow old and insist on focusing on vibrant thoughts, the signs of age won't manifest. If you dwell on thoughts of remaining robust and youthful, the body must produce corresponding results.

The elixir of youth lies in the mind or nowhere. You can't be young just by trying to appear so—you must first get rid of the last vestige of your belief that you're aging. As long as such thoughts dominate your mind, cosmetics and youthful clothing will do very little to change your appearance. You must first change your conviction that you're getting elderly in order to reverse the condition of aging. If you can establish an attitude of perpetual youth, you will have won half the battle against old age.

Some people take life too seriously and seem to think that everything depends upon their own individual efforts. Their lives are one continual grind, and their feelings are revealed in their facial expressions. Their pessimism is one of the worst enemies of youth. They age prematurely because they dwell on the depressing, diseased side of things. They dry up early in life and become wrinkled—their tissues becoming as hard as their thoughts. On the other hand, people who live on the sunny and beautiful side of life and cultivate serenity don't age nearly as rapidly.

Another reason why people age prematurely is that they cease to grow. It's a lamentable fact that so many seem incapable of accepting new ideas after they've reached middle age. They allow their mental exploration and growth to come to a standstill.

Don't think that you must stop learning just because you've gotten along in years. If you think like this, you'll decline rapidly. Never allow yourself to get out of the habit of being young. Don't say that you can't do this or that and don't be afraid of having a childlike spirit—no matter how many years you've lived. Remember that a stale mind or mentality ages the body. Keep growing and stay interested in everyone and everything around you because you can't isolate yourself without shrinking your mind.

If you wish to stay enthusiastic and vibrant, forget your unpleasant experiences. An 80-year-old lady was recently asked how she managed to keep herself so youthful. She replied, "I know how to let go of disagreeable things."

If you want to remain young, adopt the sundial's motto: "I record only the hours of sunshine." Never mind the dark or shadowed hours and forget the sad days. Remember the wonderful experiences and let the others drop into oblivion.

A man who's quite advanced in years was asked how he retains such a youthful appearance in spite of his age. He said that he's been a high-school principal for over 30 years and that he loves to stay involved in the lives and sports of young people. He keeps focused on youth, progress, and abounding life, and he doesn't have room in his mind for thoughts of old age. There isn't even a hint of infirmity in this man's conversation or ideas; in fact, there's a buoyancy about him that's wonderfully refreshing.

If you also want to keep your health and vigor, stay interested in everything, especially the hopes and ambitions of young people. When you decline to be involved with them, you're confessing that you're growing old and that your youthful spirits are drying up. "Keep growing or die" is nature's motto.

Hold firmly to the conviction that it's natural and right for you to remain active. Constantly repeat to yourself that it's wrong and wicked for you to grow old in appearance and that weakness and decrepitude couldn't have been in the Creator's plan for the humans made in His image of perfection. Repeatedly affirm: "I am always well and always young. I cannot grow old except by producing the conditions of old age through my thoughts. God intended me for continual growth and perpetual advancement, and I am not going to allow myself to be cheated out of my birthright."

Even if people say "You're getting along in years" or "You're beginning to show the signs of age," just deny these statements. Say to yourself: "I am part of the Infinite Spirit that does not age."

Never go to sleep with thoughts or images of aging in your mind because it's well known that they'll wreak havoc. It's of the utmost importance to make yourself feel young at night—to erase all convictions of age and cast aside every care and worry that would carve its image on your brain and express itself in your face. The worrying mind actually generates calcareous matter in the body and hardens the cells.

Instead, you should fall asleep holding your dearest desires uppermost in your mind. The highest possible ideals should dominate your thoughts as you drift off. As the subconscious continues to work as you slumber, these thoughts and images are intensified and increased.

When you first wake in the morning, especially if you've reached middle life or later, picture the youthful qualities as vividly possible. Say to yourself: "I am young, strong, and buoyant. I cannot grow old and decrepit because in the truth of my being, I am Divine, and Divine Principle cannot age."

We must get rid of the idea embedded in our thoughts that our bodies will inevitably wear out and become old and useless. Where did this absurd belief come from? We need to learn that living, working, and having experiences shouldn't exhaust life but create more of it. As a matter of fact, nature has bestowed upon us perpetual youth and the power of continual renewal. The body is always being regenerated. Physiologists tell us that the cells of some muscles are renewed every few days, while others are regenerated every few weeks or months. Some authorities estimate that 80 to 90 percent of all the cells in the body of the average person are entirely replaced every 6 to 24 months.

If your thoughts are focused on negative images of growing old, that image is impressed on your developing cells. In contrast, if the spirit of youth dominates your ideas, then the impression upon the cells is youthful. In short, the billions of cells composing the body are instantly affected by every thought that passes through your subconscious. It's marvelous how quickly thoughts of aging can make new cells appear old. Without realizing it, most people are using thoughts of senility and decline as a chisel that deepens their wrinkles.

Confusion, anxieties, jealousy, and the indulgence of explosive passions all tend to shorten life. People who are constantly worrying can't help but manifest problems in their bodies. Nothing in the world can counteract this ossifying process but a complete reversal of their thoughts.

Similarly, selfishness hastens aging because it violates a fundamental principle of our being: fairness. Egotism tends to rigidify and dry up the brain and nerve cells. We instinctively despise ourselves for being selfish, and this quality erodes health, harmony, and our sense of well-being.

If you want to stay young, you must learn the secret of self-rejuvenation in your thoughts. You'll find a wonderful restoring power in the cultivation of faith in the immortal Principle of health in every atom of your being. There's an aspect of yourself that never gets sick or dies: your connection with the Divine. Holding the consciousness of this great truth will heal you.

To keep from aging, you must keep the picture of youth in all its beauty and glory impressed upon your mind. Constantly affirm: "I am young because I am perpetually being renewed. My life is rejuvenated every moment by the Infinite Source of life. I am new every morning and fresh every evening because I live, move, and have my being in God."

Make this vision of continual renewal so vivid that you feel the thrill of youth throughout your entire system. Under no circumstances should you allow suggestions of old age and infirmity to creep into your mind. Remember that what you feel and are convinced of will be reflected in your body. If you think that you're getting old and walk, talk, dress, and act like an elderly person, you'll hasten the aging process.

Cling to the thought that the truth of your being can never age because it's Divine Principle. Picture the cells of the body being constantly rejuvenated, and your habit of youthful thoughts will dissolve your thought-pattern of degeneration. If you can feel your entire body being continually renewed, you'll keep it vital and young.

The elixir of youth that chemists have long sought lies in ourselves. The secret is in our own mentality, for perpetual rejuvenation is possible only by thinking correctly. Therefore, every time you think of yourself, create a vivid mental picture of your ideal self as the very image of youth, health, and vigor. Feel the spirit of youth and hope surging through your body. Form the most perfect vision of physical manhood or womanhood that's possible.

⊰✚⊱

Try to see the best in everybody. When you think of a person, hold in your mind the ideal of that individual—that which God meant him or her to be. Don't envision the deformed, weak, and ignorant creature resulting from vice and wrong living. This habit of refusing to see anything but the ideal won't only be a wonderful help to others, but also to yourself. Refuse to see defects or flaws in anyone, and persistently maintain your highest ideals.

⊰✚⊱

An all-wise and benevolent Creator wouldn't have given us such a great yearning for a long, healthy life without offering any possibility of realizing our desires. There isn't the slightest evidence that we were intended to become weak, crippled, and useless after comparatively few years. Instead, perpetual expansion and growth is our Divine destiny. "Onward and upward" is written upon every atom in the universe. Everything the Holy Deity bears the stamp of everlasting progress, and everything moves forward with Eternal purpose.

If human beings could only grasp the idea that their essence is Divine and doesn't grow old, they'd lose all sense of fear and worry, all enemies of their progress and happiness would slink away, and the aging process would cease.

⊰✚⊱

Never for a moment allow yourself to think that you're too old to do this or that, for your thoughts and convictions will very soon manifest themselves in a wrinkled face and a prematurely old expression. There's nothing more scientific than the truth that we become what we think about.

It's extremely rejuvenating to hold high ideals and lofty sentiments. The spirit can't grow old while we're constantly aspiring to something better and nobler. Let us therefore manifest beauty in our lives by thinking beautiful thoughts, envisioning glorious ideals, and picturing lovely things in our imagination.

If you want a long life, love your work and continue doing it. Don't retire at 50 because you think your powers are waning or you need a rest. Take a vacation whenever you require it, but don't give up your job. I can't grow old," says a noted actress, "because I love my art. I spend my life absorbed in it and I'm never bored. How can you develop wrinkles and become unhappy when you're always busy doing what you enjoy and your spirit is young? When I'm tired, it's not my soul that's weary but just my body."

If you don't enjoy life, feel that it's a delight to be alive, and look upon your work as a grand privilege, you'll age prematurely. Always cultivate a happy mental attitude and the aging process can't grip you. Think of Susan B. Anthony, the veteran reformer who was as vigorous and full of enthusiasm in her 80s as she was half a century earlier. And consider George Burns, who continued to perform until he died at the age of 100. Who thinks of these splendid individuals as old, failing, or left behind by younger competitors?

It's said that people who live long lives have great hopes. If you keep your spirits bright in spite of discouragements and meet all difficulties with a cheerful face, it will be extremely difficult for age to trace its furrows on your brow.

Don't let go of love or romance, for they're amulets against aging. If the mind is constantly bathed in love and filled with charitable sentiments toward all, the body will stay vibrant and healthy for many years longer than it will if the heart has dried up and been emptied of human sympathy. Compassion is the most powerful antiaging treatment and is the most exquisite of human qualities. People who would conquer the years need to avoid envy, malice, and all the small meannesses that cause bitterness in the heart, trace wrinkles on the face, and dim the eyes. A pure soul, a sound body, and a generous mind, backed by a determination to stay vibrant, constitute a fountain of youth that each of us may find in ourselves.

Think about life and express it from every pore of your being! Persistently shut the doors to all the enemies of youth—all thoughts of age and deterioration. Forget unpleasant experiences and disagreeable incidents. Through harmonious thinking, you'll retain your youthfulness and enjoy a long life.

In a Nutshell

Perfect health, vigor, and robustness are impossible to those who labor under the conviction that they're going downhill and that their powers are gradually diminishing with age.

We aren't old until our interest in life evaporates, our heart becomes unresponsive, and our spirit becomes weary. As long as we're involved in the many aspects of living, we can't grow old in spirit.

If you dwell upon the Eternal Principle and declare that your inner Divinity can't get old or die, you won't age prematurely. This habitual thought will manifest itself in the body as harmony, beauty, and grace instead of in wrinkles and the other marks of old age. You're as young as your spirit, and your face can't betray the years until the mind has given consent.

Belief is all-powerful. If you focus on thoughts of old age, old age must follow. However, if you concentrate on youthful thoughts, the body will follow suit.

Remember that a stale mind ages the body. Stay interested in everything about you. Keep growing or die!

Life should be a perpetual joy. If you don't enjoy life, feel that it's a delight to be alive, and look upon your work as a grand privilege, you'll age prematurely. Mental confusion, anxieties, jealousy, and the indulgence of explosive passions all tend to shorten life. Therefore, constantly affirm: "I am always well and always young, I cannot grow old except by producing the conditions of old age through my thought. The Creator intended me for continual growth, and I am not going to allow myself to be cheated out of my birthright of perennial youth."

Don't for a moment allow yourself to think that you're too old to do this or that, for your thoughts and convictions will very soon manifest themselves in a wrinkled face and an old expression. There's nothing more scientific than the truth that we become what we think about.

We have three qualities that will allow us to die young even if we live to be a hundred: sympathy, progress, and tolerance. The men or women who have these Divine qualities stay forever youthful.

People who want to stay young need to have compassion for everyone and avoid worry, envy, malice, and all the small meannesses that cause bitterness in the heart, trace wrinkles on the brow, and dim the eyes. A pure soul, sound body, and generous mind, backed by a determination to stay youthful, constitute a fountain of youth that each of us can find in ourselves.

Biography of Joseph Murphy

*J*oseph Murphy was born on May 20, 1898, in a small town in the County of Cork, Ireland. His father, Denis Murphy, was a deacon and professor at the National School of Ireland, a Jesuit facility. His mother, Ellen, née Connelly, was a housewife, who later gave birth to another son, John, and a daughter, Catherine.

Joseph was brought up in a strict Catholic household. His father was quite devout and, indeed, was one of the few lay professors who taught Jesuit seminarians. He had a broad knowledge of many subjects and developed in his son the desire to study and learn.

Ireland at that time was suffering from one of its many economic depressions, and many families were starving. Although Denis Murphy was steadily employed, his income was barely enough to sustain the family.

Young Joseph was enrolled in the National School and was a brilliant student. He was encouraged to study for the priesthood and was accepted as a Jesuit seminarian. However, by the time he reached his late teen years, he began to question the Catholic orthodoxy of the Jesuits, and he withdrew from the seminary. Since his goal was to explore new ideas and gain new experiences—a goal he couldn't pursue in Catholic-dominated Ireland—he left his family to go to America.

He arrived at the Ellis Island Immigration Center with only $5 in his pocket. His first project was to find a place to live. He was fortunate to locate a rooming house where he shared a room with a pharmacist who worked in a local drugstore.

Joseph's knowledge of English was minimal, as Gaelic was spoken both in his home and at school, so like most Irish immigrants, Joseph worked as a day laborer, earning enough to keep himself fed and housed.

He and his roommate became good friends, and when a job opened up at the drugstore where his friend worked, he was hired to be an assistant to the pharmacist. He immediately enrolled in a school to study pharmacy. With his keen mind and desire to learn, it didn't take long before Joseph passed the qualification exams and became a full-fledged pharmacist. He now made enough money to rent his own apartment. After a few years, he purchased the drugstore, and for the next few years ran a successful business.

When the United States entered World War II, Joseph enlisted in the Army and was assigned to work as a pharmacist in the medical unit of the 88th Infantry Division. At that time, he renewed his interest in religion and began to read extensively about various spiritual beliefs. After his discharge from the Army, he chose not to return to his career in pharmacy. He traveled extensively, taking courses in several universities both in the United States and abroad.

From his studies, Joseph became enraptured with the various Asian religions and went to India to learn about them in depth. He studied all of the major faiths and their histories. He extended these studies to the great philosophers from ancient times until the present.

Although he studied with some of the most intelligent and farsighted professors, the one person who most influenced Joseph was Dr. Thomas Troward, who was a judge as well as a philosopher, doctor, and professor. Judge Troward became Joseph's mentor and introduced him to the study of philosophy, theology, and law as well as mysticism and the Masonic order. Joseph became an active member of this order, and over the years rose in the Masonic ranks to the 32nd degree in the Scottish Rite.

Upon his return to the United States, Joseph chose to become a minister and bring his broad knowledge to the public. As his concept of Christianity was not traditional and indeed ran counter to most of the Christian denominations, he founded his own church in Los Angeles. He attracted a small number of congregants, but it did not take long for his message of optimism and hope rather than the "sin-and-damnation" sermons of so many ministers to attract many men and women to his church.

Dr. Joseph Murphy was a proponent of the New Thought movement. This movement was developed in the late 19th and early 20th centuries by many philosophers and deep thinkers who studied this phenomenon and preached, wrote, and practiced a new way of looking at life. By combining a metaphysical, spiritual, and pragmatic approach to the way we think and live, they uncovered the secret of attaining what we truly desire.

The proponents of the New Thought movement preached a new idea of life that is based on practical, spiritual principles that we can all use to enrich our lives and create perfect results. We can do these things only as we have found the law and worked out the understanding of the law, which God seems to have written in riddles in the past.

Of course, Dr. Murphy wasn't the only minister to preach this positive message. Several churches, whose ministers and congregants were influenced by the New Thought movement, were founded and developed in the decades following World War II. The Church of Religious Science, Unity Church, and other places of worship preach philosophies similar to this. Dr. Murphy named his organization The Church of Divine Science. He often shared platforms, conducted joint programs with his like-minded colleagues, and trained other men and women to join his ministry.

Over the years, other churches joined with him in developing an organization called the Federation of Divine Science, which serves as an umbrella for all Divine Science churches. Each of the Divine Science church leaders continues to push for more education, and Dr. Murphy was one of the leaders who supported the creation of the Divine Science School in St. Louis, Missouri, to train new ministers and provide ongoing education for both ministers and congregants.

The annual meeting of the Divine Science ministers was a must to attend, and Dr. Murphy was a featured speaker at this event. He encouraged the participants to study and continue to learn, particularly about the importance of the subconscious mind.

Over the next few years, Murphy's local Church of Divine Science grew so large that his building was too small to hold them. He rented The Wilshire Ebell Theater, a former movie theater. His services were so well attended that even this venue could not always accommodate all who wished to attend. Classes conducted by Dr. Murphy and his staff supplemented his Sunday services that were attended by 1,300 to 1,500 people. Seminars and lectures were held most days and evenings. The church remained at the Wilshire Ebell Theater in Los Angeles until 1976, when it moved to a new location in Laguna Hills, California.

To reach the vast numbers of people who wanted to hear his message, Dr. Murphy also created a weekly radio talk show, which eventually reached an audience of over a million listeners. Many of his followers suggested that he tape his lectures and radio programs. He was at first reluctant to do so, but agreed to experiment. His radio programs were recorded on extra-large 78-rpm discs, a common practice at that time. He had six cassettes made from one of these discs and placed them on the information table in the lobby of the Wilshire Ebell Theater. They sold out the first hour. This started a new venture. His tapes of his lectures explaining biblical texts, and providing meditations and prayers for his listeners, were not only sold in his church, but in other churches and bookstores and via mail order.

As the church grew, Dr. Murphy added a staff of professional and administrative personnel to assist him in the many programs in which he was involved and in researching and preparing his first books. One of the most effective members of his staff was his administrative secretary, Dr. Jean Wright. Their working relationship developed into a romance, and they were married—a lifelong partnership that enriched both of their lives.

At this time (the 1950s), there were very few major publishers of spiritually inspired material. The Murphys located some small publishers in the Los Angeles area, and worked with them to produce a series of small books (often 30 to 50 pages printed in pamphlet form) that were sold, mostly in churches, from $1.50 to $3.00 per book. When the orders for these books increased to the point where they required second and third printings, major publishers recognized that there was a market for such books and added them to their catalogs.

Dr. Murphy became well known outside of the Los Angeles area as a result of his books, tapes, and radio broadcasts, and was invited to lecture all over the country. He did not limit his lectures to religious matters, but spoke on the historical values of life, the art of wholesome living, and the teachings of great philosophers—from both Eastern and Western cultures.

As Dr. Murphy never learned to drive, he had to arrange for somebody to drive him to the various places where he was invited to lecture in his very busy schedule. One of Jean's functions as his administrative secretary and later as his wife was to plan his assignments and arrange for trains or flights, airport pickups, hotel accommodations, and all the other details of the trips.

The Murphys traveled frequently to many countries around the world. One of his favorite working vacations was to hold seminars on cruise ships. These trips lasted a week or more and would take him to many countries around the world. In his lectures, he emphasized the importance of understanding the power of the subconscious mind and the life principles based on belief in the one God, the "I AM."

One of Dr. Murphy's most rewarding activities was speaking to the inmates at many prisons. Many ex-convicts wrote him over the years, telling him how his words had truly turned their lives around and inspired them to live spiritual and meaningful lives.

Dr. Murphy's pamphlet-sized books were so popular that he began to expand them into more detailed and longer works. His wife gave us some insight into his manner and method of writing. She reported that he wrote his manuscripts on a tablet and pressed so hard on his pencil or pen that you could read the imprint on the next page. He seemed to be in a trance while writing. He would remain in his office for four to six hours without disturbance until he stopped and said that was enough for the day. Each day was the same. He never went back into the office again until the next morning to finish what he'd started. He took no food or drink while he was working, He was just alone with his thoughts and his huge library of books, to which he referred from time to time. His wife sheltered him from visitors and calls and took care of church business and other activities.

Dr. Murphy was always looking for simple ways to discuss the issues and to elaborate points. He chose some of his lectures to present on cassettes, records, or CDs, as technologies developed in the audio field.

His entire collection of CDs and cassettes are tools that can be used for most problems that individuals encounter in life. His basic theme is that the solution to problems lies within you. Outside elements cannot change your thinking. That is, your mind is your own. To live a better life, it's your mind, not outside circumstances, that you must change. You create your own destiny. The power of change is in your mind, and by using the power of your subconscious mind, you can make changes for the better.

Dr. Murphy wrote more than 30 books. His most famous work, *The Power of the Unconscious Mind,* which was first published in 1963, became an immediate bestseller. It was acclaimed as one of the best self-help guides ever written. Millions of copies have been sold and continue to be sold all over the world.

Among some of his other best-selling books were *Telepsychics— The Magic Power of Perfect Living, The Amazing Laws of Cosmic Mind,*

Secrets of the I-Ching, The Miracle of Mind Dynamics, Your Infinite Power to Be Rich, and *The Cosmic Power Within You.*

Dr. Murphy died in December 1981, and his wife, Dr. Jean Murphy, continued his ministry after his death. In a lecture she gave in 1986, quoting her late husband, she reiterated his philosophy:

> I want to teach men and women of their Divine Origin, and the powers regnant within them. I want to inform that this power is within and that they are their own saviors and capable of achieving their own salvation. This is the message of the Bible and nine-tenths of our confusion today is due to wrongful, literal interpretation of the life-transforming truths offered in it.
>
> I want to reach the majority, the man on the street, the woman overburdened with duty and suppression of her talents and abilities. I want to help others at every stage or level of consciousness to learn of the wonders within.

She said of her husband: "He was a practical mystic, possessed by the intellect of a scholar, the mind of a successful executive, the heart of the poet." His message summed up was: "You are the king, the ruler of your world, for you are one with God."

⁜ ⁜

Hay House Titles of Related Interest

YOU CAN HEAL YOUR LIFE, the movie,
starring Louise L. Hay & Friends
(available as a 1-DVD program and an expanded 2-DVD set)
Watch the trailer at: **www.LouiseHayMovie.com**

❦

*CALM: A Proven Four-Step Process Designed Specifically for
Women Who Worry,* by Denise Marek

*THE POWER OF A SINGLE THOUGHT: How to Initiate Major Life
Changes from the Quiet of Your Mind* (book-with-CD),
revised and edited by Gay Hendricks and Debbie DeVoe

*THE POWER OF INTENTION: Learning to Co-create Your World
Your Way,* by Dr. Wayne W. Dyer

*10 STEPS TO TAKE CHARGE OF YOUR EMOTIONAL LIFE:
Overcoming Anxiety, Distress, and Depression Through
Whole-Person Healing,* by Eve A. Wood, M.D.

*WHAT TO DO WHEN YOU DON'T KNOW WHAT TO DO:
Common Horse Sense,* by Wyatt Webb

❦

All of the above are available at your local
bookstore, or may be ordered by contacting:

Hay House USA: **www.hayhouse.com**®
Hay House Australia: **www.hayhouse.com.au**
Hay House UK: **www.hayhouse.co.uk**
Hay House South Africa: **www.hayhouse.co.za**
Hay House India: **www.hayhouse.co.in**

Notes

Notes

Notes

Notes

Notes

Notes

Notes

Notes

Notes

Notes

Notes

Notes

Notes

We hope you enjoyed this Hay House book.
If you'd like to receive a free catalog featuring additional
Hay House books and products, or if you'd like information about the
Hay Foundation, please contact:

Hay House, Inc.
P.O. Box 5100
Carlsbad, CA 92018-5100

(760) 431-7695 or **(800) 654-5126**
(760) 431-6948 (fax) or **(800) 650-5115 (fax)**
www.hayhouse.com® • **www.hayfoundation.org**

⌖

Published and distributed in Australia by: Hay House Australia Pty. Ltd.,
18/36 Ralph St., Alexandria NSW 2015 • *Phone:*
612-9669-4299 • *Fax:* 612-9669-4144 • www.hayhouse.com.au

Published and distributed in the United Kingdom by: Hay House UK, Ltd.,
292B Kensal Rd., London W10 5BE • *Phone:* 44-20-8962-1230
Fax: 44-20-8962-1239 • www.hayhouse.co.uk

Published and distributed in the Republic of South Africa by: Hay House SA
(Pty), Ltd., P.O. Box 990, Witkoppen 2068 • *Phone/Fax:* 27-11-467-8904
orders@psdprom.co.za • www.hayhouse.co.za

Published in India by: Hay House Publishers India, Muskaan
Complex, Plot No. 3, B-2, Vasant Kunj, New Delhi 110 070
Phone: 91-11-4176-1620 • *Fax:* 91-11-4176-1630 • www.hayhouse.co.in

Distributed in Canada by: Raincoast, 9050 Shaughnessy St.,
Vancouver, B.C. V6P 6E5 • *Phone:* (604) 323-7100
Fax: (604) 323-2600 • www.raincoast.com

⌖

Tune in to **HayHouseRadio.com**® for the best in inspirational talk
radio featuring top Hay House authors! And, sign up via the Hay House
USA Website to receive the Hay House online newsletter and stay informed
about what's going on with your favorite authors. You'll receive bimonthly
announcements about: Discounts and Offers, Special Events, Product
Highlights, Free Excerpts, Giveaways, and more!
www.hayhouse.com®